PARENTAL DISCIPLINARY STRATEGIES AND

THE CHILD'S MORAL INTERNALIZATION

PARENTAL DISCIPLINARY STRATEGIES AND

THE CHILD'S MORAL INTERNALIZATION

Een wetenschappelijke proeve op het gebied van de sociale wetenschappen

PROEFSCHRIFT

ter verkrijging van de graad van doctor
aan de Katholieke Universiteit te Nijmegen,
volgens besluit van het college van decanen
in het openbaar te verdedigen op
dinsdag 5 februari 1991, des namiddags te 3.30 uur.

door

Antonia Johanna Elisabeth de Veer

geboren op 7 juni 1959 te Eindhoven

Promotor: Prof. dr. J.R.M. Gerris

Co-promotor: Dr. J.M.A.M. Janssens

ISBN: 90-9003891-4
Copyright: A.J.E. de Veer
Druk: Druk & Vorm

ACKNOWLEDGEMENTS

A research project cannot be carried out without the support and cooperation of persons. Particularly the cooperation of the teachers, pupils, and parents was important to the research.

Interviewing the pupils and parents and transcribing these interviews require considerable support of others. I owe a great deal to those who in these have contributed to my investigations. Without their contribution this study would have been impossible.

The discussions with my colleagues provided valuable stimulation, both theoretically and methodologically. Several of my colleagues and assistants within the Institute of Family Studies of the Catholic University of Nijmegen contributed a lot to the progress of the project and to publishing its results. I appreciate their encouragement, suggestions, and help. I truly enjoyed working with them.

I am very grateful to Jan Gerris and Jan Janssens for their faith in me. Jan Gerris was always willing to suggest new ideas. Most of all, I wish to thank Jan Janssens for his support at times when the obstacles seemed insurmountable and for his optimism.

I am thankful to L. Weeks, who with great skill and speed corrected this dissertation in grammar and style. All remaining mistakes are mine.

Last I am grateful to Margot Fleuren, who does not want to be thanked, but deserves it. With her involvement, humor, and relativism she contributed greatly to the realization of this dissertation.

November, 1990
Nijmegen

TABLE OF CONTENTS

1   INTRODUCTION

In 1963 Hoffman claimed that no single piece of research can supply the answers to the important questions in complex areas such as morality and its antecedents (Hoffman, 1963). Now, more than a quarter of a century later, this assertion is still valid. This study, therefore, is intended to shed light on a small facet of moral internalization.

Because the theoretical considerations are primarily based on Martin Hoffman's theory, moral internalization will be defined in accord with Hoffman's formulation. Care of others is the focus of Hoffman's moral theory (Hoffman, 1987), and he defined a moral norm as considering the needs of others (Hoffman, 1983). According to Hoffman (1970) this norm is initially alien. The young child is motivated only by hedonistic needs. The origin of these hedonistic needs may be largely constitutional (Hoffman, 1975a). In a moral encounter, there is a conflict between the child's own hedonistic needs and the needs of another person. When the child has not yet internalized the moral norm to take the needs of another person into account, such a conflict may be induced by another person, such as the caretaker. When the norm is internalized, the child's behavior is accordingly guided even when an external authority is not present to enforce the norm. In other words, the development of the motivation to control hedonistic needs for social purposes is hypothesized to be the outcome of socialization.

Just what kind of socialization experiences may be of importance for this internalization process? Hoffman suggested that the way in which parents discipline (i.e., the strategy used to change the child's behavior) may be crucial. On the one hand, inductive techniques such as pointing out the consequences of the child's behavior for the other person, stimulating the child to place him- or herself in the other's position, or giving explanations should promote children to take another's needs into account. On the other hand, trying to influence the children's behavior primarily by asserting power (e.g., punishing the child) is expected to focus children on their own position rather than the situation of others. Relations between parental discipline and moral internalization are frequently found, indicating that Hoffman's presupposition may make sense (for reviews see Hoffman, 1963, 1970; Rollins & Thomas, 1979; Shaffer & Brody, 1981; and section 3.3.1 below).

Using Hoffman's theory, the present study is intended to shed light on the relation between parental discipline strategies and the child's moral internalization. Two problems will be studied. The first problem concerns the relation between parental discipline and the child's internalization of norms focusing on the problem of 'who is influencing whom?' This topic is rather traditional (see Bell, 1968, 1977; Clarke-Stewart, 1988; Hoffman, 1975a; Lewis, 1981), but nevertheless relevant because of the various unresolved issues.

1

Hoffman assumed the child's moral internalization to be primarily influenced by the way parents discipline. In contrast, it can be argued that the extent to which children have internalized norms (i.e., the extent to which children are motivated to consider another's need) influences the strategies used by parents. Hoffman (1975a), however, argued parental discipline to most likely influence long-term moral internalization rather than the reverse.

Many studies relating parent and child variables are strictly correlational, leaving the problem of causal direction unresolved (Bell, 1968; Hoffman, 1975a). Some studies, however, have investigated the effects children exert on parents and/or parents on children. In a recently published review, Clarke-Stewart (1988) concluded that we can no longer make simple generalizations about the one-sided effects of parental discipline on child behavior and development. The question of who influences whom when discipline and moral internalization are concerned nevertheless remains unanswered. This is in part because studies designed to make inferences about the causality of parent-child interactions have primarily referred to short-term interactions (e.g., Brunk & Henggeler, 1984; Chapman, 1979; Yarrow, Waxler & Scott, 1971) or infants (e.g., Clarke-Stewart, 1973; Clarke-Stewart & Hevey, 1981). In addition, variables that are not of direct relevance to the issue of moral internalization are often employed. For example, person orientation (Keller & Bell, 1979), responsiveness (Bugental, Caporael & Shennum, 1980) or compliance (Lytton, 1979) are among the variables typically studied.

The second problem to be studied concerns the role of the child's empathy and perspective taking in the relation between parental discipline and moral internalization. According to Hoffman (1987), empathy may provide the basis for a comprehensive theory of moral internalization. Empathy is defined as an affective response that is more appropriate to someone else's situation than to one's own (e.g., Hoffman, 1983, 1987). Hoffman suggested that empathy and perspective taking are critical to the internalization of norms. Empathy may motivate the child to take the needs of the other into account. Whether or not empathy is such a motive depends on the subjective experience of empathy. This subjective experience of empathy is not stable but is related to the child's cognitive sense of others. Hoffman (1984a, 1987) assumed the child to have an inborn capacity to react affectively to another person. When confronted with another's emotions the child reacts affectively. An infant is initially unable to distinguish between another's distress and one's own feeling of distress. An infant who reacts with empathy is not aware that another person and not the self is in distress. Even the young child (until approximately 2 or 3-years-old) may not realize that the cause of the experienced feelings of distress is the distress of the other person and it is therefore unlikely that the child would offer help. When the child realizes, perhaps as a consequence of the growing ability to take perspectives, that the experience of distress is actually a reaction to the other's distress, the child may become motivated to help the other person. This suggests that the development of empathic distress corresponds with the development of perspective taking.

Particular discipline strategies may stimulate the child to react empathically and, at the same time, stimulate the child's perspective-taking ability. According to Hoffman's information-processing approach to moral internalization, discipline influences both the child's affective and cognitive processes (e.g., 1975b, 1982a, 1983, 1984a). As far as we know, however, Hoffman's hypothesis that empathy and perspective taking mediate between parental discipline and moral internalization has not been tested.

As already mentioned, only a small facet of morality will be studied based on Martin Hoffman's theory of the development of moral internalization. We focus on two key issues: the causality problem and the role of empathy and perspective taking when parental discipline strategies influence the child's moral internalization. Various aspects will not be investigated. First, only relations between parents and children are treated. We are aware that this is just a part of the broader system in which children and parents live. Socialization by siblings, peers, teachers, television programs etc., is omitted. Moreover, the interaction is simplified by primarily referring to parent-child pairs. So we focus on parent-child socialization.

Second, we focus on the relation between parental discipline strategies and moral internalization, even though there are many more variables that might be critical to the child's moral internalization. The child's temperament, for example, may influence both the discipline strategies parents use and the child's moral internalization (Belsky, 1984). A variable which may mediate between parental discipline and the child's moral internalization is the child's identification with the parent (Hoffman, 1971a). Because of the emphasis Hoffman put on empathy and the close relationship between empathy and perspective taking, only the role of empathy and perspective taking will be examined in this study.

A third factor that should be kept in mind but will not be directly examined here is the possibility of other variables influencing parental discipline. Just as there are numerous variables determining the child's moral internalization, there are also numerous determinants of individual differences in parental functioning. Parental child-rearing practices may not only be influenced by the child's moral internalization, but also by the personality of the parent, marital relations, and the surrounding social network (Belsky, 1984). The present research focuses exclusively on the interaction between the child's moral internalization and parental discipline, leaving other determinants of parenting aside.

Fourth, we are not interested in interactions at a microanalytic level (e.g., analyzing the parent-child interaction from a single, brief observational session in fine detail). The present study, rather, applies a broader perspective to parent-child interaction, examining interactions over an extended period of time. Repeated observations will be analyzed to unravel the causal relations between discipline strategies employed by the parents and the moral internalization of the child. Repeated observations will also be used to show both stability in the kind of discipline strategies used and the moral internalization of the child.

In summary, the aim of this study is to test part of Hoffman's theory of moral internalization. First, the directionality of the relation between parental discipline and moral internalization will be examined in chapter 2. Hoffman's rationale for why discipline should most likely be the antecedent to moral internalization will be outlined. Then, it will be argued that it is nevertheless possible for the child to influence parental reactions, suggesting a bidirectional model. The chapter is concluded by summarizing methodological consequences for the study of the directionality problem. In chapter 3 the way in which the child's ability to react empathically to others and perspective-taking capacity might mediate between discipline and moral internalization is discussed. In chapter 4 the hypotheses to be tested in the present study will be outlined. The procedures and research methods used in this study are described in chapter 5. In chapter 6 the results of our research are reported and in chapter 7 the results are interpreted and evaluated.

2 PARENTAL DISCIPLINE: ANTECEDENT OR CONSEQUENCE OF MORAL INTERNALIZATION

Central to this chapter is the relation between discipline and moral internalization. Hoffman presupposed that parental discipline strategies will have a crucial effect on the child's moral internalization. Before discussing this presupposition (section 2.2), however, we must first describe discipline more precisely and why Hoffman hypothesized parental discipline to be so important for moral internalization (section 2.1). We will then consider his arguments in more detail and an alternative, namely that parental discipline strategies might be a consequence of the child's level of moral internalization (section 2.3). A design intended to examine the long-term effects of parental discipline on moral internalization will then be presented (section 2.4).

2.1 Discipline and its importance to moral internalization

Hoffman claimed that parental discipline strategies play a central role in the internalization of moral norms (Hoffman, 1963, 1970). Parents obviously use discipline techniques to attempt to change the child's behavior in the direction desirable to the parents.

It should be noted, however, that Hoffman considered discipline in particular situations in where the parent attempts to change the child's behavior against the child's will (e.g., Hoffman, 1983). Discipline strategies apply to many different situations. For example, the parent may simply want the child involved in a different activity, such as going to bed rather than watching TV (Hoffman, 1975a). The parent may want to teach the child the conventions of etiquette (e.g., "don't eat with your fingers"). Or, in other situations, the parent may want the child to help another child (e.g., "she cannot do it by herself, she is too little"). These situations were referred to by Hoffman as "discipline encounters". In theoretical considerations, however, Hoffman focused on those discipline encounters that involved a moral norm (Hoffman, 1983). In the present study, therefore, discipline is exclusively related to situations in which the child is going to transgress a norm or already has transgressed a norm. That is, a narrow definition of discipline encounter is used, referring only to moral situations. Hoffman admitted that information about moral norms and messages regarding how the child should act are communicated to the child outside the discipline encounter (e.g., in table conversations, television programs, and by the parent's own actions). Nevertheless, Hoffman considered discipline encounters in particular to be crucial to moral internalization.

It should be noted that an attempt to change the child's behavior against the child's will does not imply that the child necessarily intended to harm another person or wanted to fulfill some hedonistic needs. In discipline encounters parents simply encourage their children to consider the needs of others.

Three discipline categories can be distinguished (Hoffman, 1970; Hoffman & Saltzstein, 1967; Rollins & Thomas, 1979):

1. Induction refers to techniques in which the parent gives explanations or reasons for requiring the child to change his behavior (e.g., by pointing out the painful consequences of the child's behavior for others). The parent attempts to induce the child to voluntarily comply.

2. Power assertion can be defined as behavior that results in considerable external pressure on the child to behave according to the parent's desires. It includes physical punishment, deprivation of material objects or privileges, the direct application of force, or the threat of any of these. Rather than rely on the child's inner resources (e.g., empathy, guilt, shame, love) or provide the child with information necessary for the development of such resources, the parent punishes the child physically or materially, or relies on the child's fear of punishment.

3. Love withdrawal is defined as nonphysical expression of the parent's anger or disapproval of the child with the implication that love will not be restored until the child behaves in accordance with the parent's wishes (e.g., ignoring, isolating, or rejecting the child).[1]

Parental control attempts (i.e., discipline) is one of the variables that Rollins and Thomas (1979) identified as critical to the socialization of children. The second variable is parental support, which refers to parental behavior that makes the child feel comfortable in the presence of the parent. The child feels accepted and approved of by the parent as a person (Rollins & Thomas, 1979).

There seems to be ample evidence for a positive relationship between parental support and aspects of moral development (Rollins & Thomas, 1979; Shaffer & Brody, 1981; Zahn-Waxler, Radke-Yarrow & King, 1979). There is also some evidence that any type of discipline may be more effective when administered in a warm, affectionate context (Shaffer & Brody, 1981).

Hoffman highlighted the potential relevance of parental warmth by pointing out its ability to promote identification, make the child more receptive to discipline, make the child more likely to imitate the parent, and make the child emotionally secure enough to be open to the needs of others (Hoffman, 1963, 1979). Notwithstanding the influence of parental warmth and other socialization

---

[1] Originally, love withdrawal and induction belonged to one broad category "psychological discipline" because both techniques motivated the child to change his future behavior (Hoffman, 1963). Later this category was divided into induction and love withdrawal (Hoffman & Saltzstein, 1967).

experiences, the discipline strategies parents choose are dominant in influencing the child's moral internalization according to Hoffman (1983).

Why should discipline be so important? Central to Hoffman's argument is his characterization of moral internalization. Moral internalization in Hoffman's view consists of considering the needs of others (e.g., Hoffman, 1963, 1975a). A child has internalized this norm when the child experiences a conflict between the moral requirements of the situation and his own hedonistic desires. Because the origin of hedonistic needs may be largely constitutional, moreover, development of the motivation to control these hedonistic desires for social purposes must be a product of socialization.

What past experiences might make a person particularly sensitive to such a moral conflict? According to Hoffman this sensitivity to moral conflicts is associated with the kind of experiences one had when faced with the same conflict. That is, a conflict between one's desires at a given moment and the norm to consider the needs of the other. The norm is initially external. The norm is embedded in the many physical and verbal messages from the parent regarding how the child should act. In discipline encounters, moreover, this moral conflict may be raised by the use of inductive messages. It is mainly in the discipline encounter that the connection is made between the norms, the child's egoistic desires, and the child's behavior (Hoffman, 1975a, 1983, 1984b).

A second factor that may make discipline so critical to children's awareness of a moral conflict is their active involvement in the conflict (Hoffman, 1983, 1984b). The child is the interested party and involved as an actor in the conflict at the same time. The message of the parent, embedded in the discipline technique, is meaningfully related to the child's ongoing activity and therefore may be better processed and remembered in the future.

Aside from these theoretical reasons for expecting discipline situations to be important for moral internalization, Hoffman also mentioned empirical evidence that discipline is a recurrent salient feature in the child's daily life. Young children (i.e., children 2-10 years of age) appear to experience pressure from parents to change their behavior every 6 to 7 minutes on the average throughout their waking hours. In other words, these situations occur so often that it seems reasonable to assume that the type of discipline used by parents will affect the child's moral internalization (Hoffman, 1983, 1984b). In most of these instances, moreover, the child does end up complying.

Although Hoffman frequently relied on these data concerning the frequency of discipline encounters, this argument may not be as convincing as it seems to be. When Hoffman cited studies of the frequency of discipline encounters he does not pay attention to the particular kind of behavior being performed by the child. Studies indicate that moral situations (e.g., harm another or help another) constitute a conceptual and developmental system distinct from situations concerning social conventions (more or less arbitrary rules such as table manners) (Turiel & Smetana, 1984). It can be hypothesized, thus, that parents react differently when they perceive the child's behavior as a moral transgression or a conventional

7

transgression. Gerris, Vermulst and Franken (1988) asked parents of 4 to 18-year-olds to describe those child-rearing interactions that frequently caused a conflict between the parent and the child. Only 33% of the situations parents mentioned referred to transgressions of norms and rules, such as social conventions. Thus, discipline encounters that involve a moral norm in the more restricted sense might be much less than every 6 to 7 minutes.

In sum, notwithstanding the fact that the relevance of every disciplinary action to moral internalization can be questioned, the similarity between a moral discipline encounter and an internal moral encounter is crucial for Hoffman to stress the importance of parental discipline strategies for in the child's internalization of norms.

2.2   Discipline as an antecedent to moral internalization

Many authors consider socialization as an adult initiated process by which children acquire norms (Bell, 1968). According to Baumrind (1980) children, by virtue of their immaturity and dependent status, do not have the same contribution to the interaction as parents. Caretakers play a dominant role in the way their children develop. Maccoby and Martin (1983), for example, also believed that when the infant is quite young, the mother shapes the infant's behavior to a greater extent than the infant influences the mother's behavior. Developmental changes in the parent-child relationship may involve a shift of regulatory functions from the parent to the child. According to others the unilateral relation between parent and child is crucial (e.g., Piaget, 1965; Youniss, 1980). Such a unilateral relation means that, although the parent-child interaction includes a two-way flow, the child must also make unilateral adjustments. That is, adults bring in their viewpoint based on their own experiences to the situation and are not ready to abandon this viewpoint for the relatively inexperienced view of the child.

In Hoffman's view, as well, it is more likely that parental discipline is the antecedent and not a consequence of the child's moral internalization. Hoffman did not deny that children often affect their parents' behavior, particularly in short-range day-to-day interactions. Nevertheless, parental discipline is more likely to be the antecedent than the consequence of children's long-term moral internalization, argued Hoffman (1975a), and central in this argument is the concept of power (Hoffman, 1975a).

Power is the potential an individual A has for compelling individual B to behave in a way contrary to B's desires (Hoffman, 1975a). The parent has total control over the child's material and emotional supplies. Other institutions (e.g., the law) exercise little constraint in this domain and the parent therefore has a great deal of power over the child. This power, moreover, plays a crucial role in encounters where the parent wants to change the child's behavior. The parent decides how to react and chooses the discipline strategies accordingly. The parent may directly assert his or her power (i.e., apply external pressure on the child to comply) or may choose techniques intended to gain 'voluntary' behavior change by eliciting internal forces in the child. Even in cases where the child has a certain amount of behavioral freedom, this freedom depends entirely on how much the parent is willing to allow the child.

In sum, the parent has an overwhelming amount of control over the parent-child interaction and the amount of influence a child can exert on this interaction depends on the permissiveness of the parent.

Hoffman tried to further underscore his argument by reasoning from the opposite perspective as well (see, for example, Hoffman, 1975a, 1960, 1970). If moral internalization precedes parental discipline then parental discipline should not only relate to the degree of moral internalization exhibited at school but, above all, to the degree of moral internalization manifested at home. For this reason Hoffman (1960) studied the relation between the child's resistance to the mother and the mother's disciplinary strategy. Despite the positive relation between power assertion and the child's aggressiveness at school, Hoffman found no relation between power assertion and rebelliousness at home. Therefore he concluded parental discipline does not follow from moral internalization. Other findings, however, are in disagreement with this research: Hoffman and Saltzstein (1967), for example, found a relation between the child's overt reaction to transgression at home and discipline.

A second consequence of assuming that the child's moral internalization influences discipline (rather than the reverse) is that another theory is then required to explain the development of moral internalization itself. Here Hoffman confined himself to the relation between inductive discipline and moral internalization. Hoffman (1975a) offered three possibilities promoting moral internalization. Subsequently, however, he rejected all three alternatives on the basis of empirical or logical reasons and adopted the assumption that moral internalization is a consequence of discipline. The first alternative stimulator of moral internalization Hoffman suggested was that a parent who uses induction also often uses love withdrawal. Love withdrawal may produce anxiety over loss of parental love, which promotes the child's moral internalization. Thus love withdrawal and not inductive discipline may cause moral internalization. According to Hoffman there is no evidence to support this hypothesis. No consistent relations are found between love withdrawal and moral internalization (Hoffman, 1975a). Second, Hoffman proposed that the child's identification with the parent may lead to adoption of the parent's moral orientation. This hypothesis is rejected because empirical research appears not to verify the existence of a relationship between the child's identification with the parent and the child's moral internalization. The final alternative Hoffman put forward to explain the emergence of moral internalization is that an exposure to levels of moral reasoning that are moderately higher than one's current level may result in moral internalization. Hoffman mentioned several arguments why this hypothesis may not be relevant. One argument is that this is a purely cognitive hypothesis and says nothing about noncognitive aspects of morality.

Even if moral internalization should be caused by variables other than discipline, this does not necessarily relate to the causal relation between discipline and moral internalization. Bell (1977), for example, suggested that a child-effect on the process of moral internalization need not imply that the child's moral internalization produces the parental technique.

Hoffman (1975a) also verified his theory of moral internalization as a consequence of parental discipline with his own empirical research bearing on the basis of parental discipline choice. Parents view their techniques as deriving from considerations outside the child's control (e.g., the parents' long-term goals). In addition to his findings that parents viewed themselves as the original source for using a particular technique, parental attributes such as educational level, parental values, and marital relationship were also found to influence the discipline technique used by parents (Hoffman, 1975a).

As a second source of empirical evidence, Hoffman (1975a) referred to several studies on the frequency of discipline encounters. He concluded that parents attempt to influence the child four to five times as often as the child attempts to dominate the parent. Furthermore, parents do usually have their way when they wish to change their child's behavior. As already mentioned in the previous section, however, this evidence is not particularly compelling because the specific content of the conflict was not taken into account.

In addition to Hoffman's arguments, other research has also indicated that parental behavior towards their children is often affected by variables other than the children themselves. In Belsky's process model of parenting the parent's personality, marital relation, developmental history, and social network are also seen as some of the determinants of parenting (Belsky, 1984). In a longitudinal study on determinants of parenting, moreover, it was found that the child-rearing experienced by the parents themselves and the parent's personality influenced their later interactions with their own children (Belsky, Hertzog & Rovine, 1986).

Other studies suggesting that parental discipline precedes moral internalization are studies reporting correlations between parental beliefs and their discipline technique (Janssens & Gerris, 1988), although this does not exclude the interpretation that beliefs are a justification for action (Goodnow, 1988). Furthermore, correlations have been found between the moral reasoning of the child and parental moral reasoning (Haan, Langer & Kohlberg, 1976; Buck, Walsh & Rothman, 1981) and between parental moral reasoning and child-rearing method (Buck, Walsh & Rothman, 1981). It is likely that parental moral reasoning influences the child-rearing method rather than the reverse. Thus, these findings also suggest that parental behavior is affected by variables that are not under the control of the child and that the child's moral reasoning is influenced by the parent.

10

Despite the influences on parenting that lie outside the child's control, discipline need not be the antecedent to moral internalization. Stated differently, if it is true that parental discipline is influenced by a number of variables on which children cannot exert any influence, it is still possible that parental discipline is also influenced by child variables such as moral internalization. Furthermore, it does not rule out the possibility that moral internalization is best described with a reciprocal influence model. In addition to the parental characteristics that may influence discipline strategies, child effects on parental discipline may also have to be taken into consideration. In the next section, therefore, the research to child effects on adult discipline will be reviewed.

2.3   Discipline as a consequence of moral internalization

In 1968 Bell criticized much of the work done in this area because of its unilateral perspective. Bell pointed out that many of the findings that had been interpreted as evidence of parental effects on the child's functioning could logically be construed as child effects on parenting. Adults not only socialize children but children also socialize adults. Bell assumed that parents do not have fixed techniques for socializing children. They have a repertoire of actions and different children trigger different actions. Bell highlighted congenital influences (e.g., the child's aggressiveness, competence and social responsivity) because they clearly emanate from the child. But child effects on parental behavior are not just a consequence of congenital and genetic factors (Bell, 1968, 1971, 1977). Bell argued that child behavior influences the parent, whatever the origin of the behavior is.

Thus, whereas Hoffman proposed a unidirectional model, Bell stressed a bidirectional model and attempted to explain and predict adult-child interaction in terms of reciprocal effects.

Using the aforementioned statement of congenital influences, Bell (1968) also gave an alternative interpretation of the findings of Hoffman. Bell's supposition was that the children showing little moral internalization are congenitally low in person orientation. They respond less to rather subtle hints, demands, and expressions of love of the parents than children high in person orientation. Because of this unresponsiveness to social stimuli their parents will be less affectionate and do not appeal to the child's personal or social values with inductive discipline.

Hoffman (1975a, 1983) has admitted that the parent-child interaction can be influenced by factors such as the aggressive tendencies in the child, the child's person orientation, the emotional attitude toward the parent, and the level of cognitive development. However, these child characteristics are not the same as moral internalization. Although these factors may affect parental discipline strategies this does not invalidate the argument that parental discipline is an antecedent of moral internalization.

11

This distinction between congenital child characteristics and moral internalization is also made by Belsky (1984). In Belsky's model child characteristics influence child development as well as parental discipline. However, parental discipline is also assumed to directly influence the child's development.

A second conclusion of Bell, interfacing with Hoffman's concept of power, is that the relation between parent and child might be reciprocal despite the inequality of maturity (Bell, 1977). Bell agreed with Hoffman that parents have the physical size and control of resources to determine the outcome of an interaction more often than the child. But, as Bell argued, this dominance is not completely onesided. Children start approximately 50% of the interactions and also dominate a substantial number of interactions. They can get their way by their appealing nature and can exercise a steady and persistent resistance to the parent's objectives (Bell, 1977).

Support for Bell's viewpoint comes from observations of adult-child interactions that indicate that the adults' responses to children vary with the responses the children bring to a given situation (e.g., Anderson, Lytton & Romney, 1986; Yarrow, Waxler & Scott, 1971). Yarrow, Waxler and Scott (1971) trained adults to play a high- or a low-nurturance role with small groups of children. In spite of this training the adult's responsiveness varied with child variables such as the child's attention-seeking behavior and friendly or aggressive interactions with their peers.

Bell (1977) used studies on the relative frequency of interaction initiation to demonstrate the child's influence. Studies on this subject must be interpreted with caution, however. Maccoby and Martin (1983) concluded from observations of parent-infant interactions that there is probably no general answer to the question of which member of the mother-child pair is more likely to initiate the interaction. The balance depends heavily on the situational characteristics such as the parent's engagement in another task (e.g., cooking).

In summary, Bell criticized the unidirectional model of Hoffman by pointing out the influences of, particularly congenital, child factors on parental behavior and by weakening the claim that parents have much more power in the interaction than children.

Whereas Bell's arguments are primarily logical and empirical, showing that children can influence parental behavior, Hoffman might still argue that the crux of the whole matter is not the possible influence of other child characteristics on parental discipline but the influence of moral internalization on parental discipline. Can theoretical arguments be found for the thesis that parental discipline is a consequence of moral internalization?

Saltzstein (1976) proposed a model of how moral internalization may influence parental discipline based on the parallel between theories of social influence processes and Kohlberg's levels of moral development. He suggested that the moral development of the child may determine the social influences to which the child is susceptible, which in turn shape the kind of discipline the parents use. For example, children who conform to moral rules for extrinsic reasons are primarily susceptible to social influence aimed at compliance and therefore elicit various forms of power assertion from their parents. Whereas children who conform to moral rules based on concern for the welfare of others (the norm is internalized according to Hoffman) are susceptible to social influence designed to be internally consistent with one's own values. These children elicit reasoning and other principled appeals from their parents. Saltzstein concluded that the process is best conceived as circular: the moral development of the child determines his susceptibility to different discipline techniques and these techniques, in turn, influence the child's moral development.

In sum, Hoffman's hypothesis that the discipline techniques parents use with children constitute an antecedent to long-term moral internalization has neither been confirmed nor rejected. Pros and cons were pointed out, but further research is clearly needed to unravel who is influencing whom in the domain of parental discipline and moral internalization.

2.4   The problem of causal directionality

As outlined in the preceding section, Hoffman's thesis that parental discipline is the antecedent to moral internalization has been criticized heavily on logical, empirical and theoretical grounds. A bidirectional model seems obvious. Although the study of a parent-child bidirectional model has found many advocates, very few data have been collected or published within a bidirectional model. The first aim in this study, thus, is to find evidence for Hoffman's presupposition that parental discipline precedes moral internalization.

How can Hoffman's thesis be examined? First, Hoffman's thesis concerns long-term effects of parental discipline on moral internalization. Experimental laboratory studies and sequential analyses usually focus on short-term interaction. Chapman (1981) illustrated that isolation of short-term causal effects may yield results different from those reached by the isolation of long-term effects. Second, because Hoffman rejected the influence of congenital factors on discipline as a falsification of his thesis, parental discipline and moral internalization must be the main variables. Third, Hoffman's theory refers to global disciplinary strategies and global measures of moral internalization. Yarrow, Waxler and Scott (1971), however, have pointed out the importance of distinguishing global traits from direct interaction characteristics because it may yield different results. Fourth, Hoffman stated that parental influence on children is stronger than the influence of children on their parents. Thus, the design should permit inferences about the relative strength of child effects and parent effects. Finally, Hoffman (1970) preferred naturalistic research, keeping us closer to real life concepts.

Keeping the above-mentioned items in mind, a panel design was used. This design has been recommended by several authors working on the relation between parental discipline and moral internalization because it allows inferences to be drawn over time (cf. Hoffman, 1979; Maccoby & Martin, 1983; Saltzstein,

1976; Shaffer & Brody, 1981). In this panel design the behavior of both participants (parent and child) is assessed at two measurement periods. Measures of parental discipline obtained at time 1 can then be related with indicators of the child's moral internalization at time 2, providing a measure of the contribution of discipline to moral internalization. Conversely, measures of the child's moral internalization obtained at the beginning of the interval can be related to measures of parental discipline at the end of the interval in order to obtain a measure of the impact of the child on parental discipline. If a significant relation between parental discipline at time 1 and the child's moral internalization at time 2 emerges, this fact alone does not justify an inference of a cross time causal relationship between the two measures. The relation may be spurious because it may reflect a relation between the parent's discipline strategies at time 1 and the child's moral internalization at time 1 combined with a simple continuation of the child's moral internalization from time 1 to time 2. Similarly, a significant relation between the child's moral internalization at time 1 and the parent's disciplinary strategies at time 2 may be the product of a cross-sectional relation between the child's moral internalization and parental discipline at time 1 and a stability of parental discipline from time 1 to time 2. An analysis of all relations between parental discipline strategies and the child's moral internalization assessed at two occasions will probably shed more light on the long-term effect of parental discipline and moral internalization.

The second aim of this study is to examine the mechanism hypothesized by Hoffman to influence the internalization of norms. Hoffman assumed that moral internalization is the consequence of parental discipline. He hypothesized that parental discipline may influence the child's moral internalization by stimulating the child's perspective taking within the moral encounter and by arousing empathy within the child. The mediating role of perspective taking and empathy in the relationship between parental disciplinary strategies and the child's moral internalization will therefore be described in the next chapter.

3   THE INFLUENCE OF PARENTAL DISCIPLINE ON CHILDREN'S MORAL INTERNALIZATION

Discussing the direction of the relation between parental discipline and moral internalization does not isolate the way in which discipline techniques relate to moral internalization. It will be hypothesized that parents influence the child's empathy and perspective-taking capacity with their disciplinary strategies and that these empathic and perspective-taking capabilities further influence the child's moral internalization. In the discipline encounter the parent tries to control the child's behavior. In chapter 2 (section 2.1) we distinguished between induction, power assertion, and withdrawal of love as three techniques a parent may use to achieve a behavioral change. In this chapter we will further elaborate Hoffman's theory on moral internalization in order to isolate the mechanisms responsible for the influence of discipline on moral internalization. Thus, although we do not preclude the possibility that moral internalization also influences discipline, we further confine ourselves to only a consideration of how discipline can affect internalization.

As Hoffman (1983) noted, moral internalization means different things in different theoretical contexts. Before giving a theoretical explanation of how norms may become internalized, therefore, a description of the concept of moral internalization will be given (section 3.1). Hoffman's theoretical formulation of how discipline influences moral internalization will then be outlined (section 3.2) and research on the relation between discipline techniques and moral internalization briefly summarized (section 3.3).

3.1   Moral internalization

Of central importance in theories of moral development is the definition of the concept of moral internalization. Many approaches to moral internalization exist, such as the psychoanalytic view (see Hoffman, 1970), the behavioristic view (e.g., Aronfreed, 1976), and the cognitively oriented stage theories of Piaget and Kohlberg (e.g., Kohlberg, 1976; Piaget, 1965). Every approach has its own conception of morality and this conception of course influences further theorizing about moral development. This will be illustrated in the following, using the theories of Kohlberg and Piaget.

Kohlberg stressed the cognitive-structural component of moral development. He identified morality with justice and his theory concentrates on the development of cognitive justice structures. The different moral stages reflect the different types of relationships between the self and society's rules and expectations (Kohlberg, 1976) and Kohlberg is concerned with the development of moral reasoning in particular. As a result of the interactions with the environment the child's reasoning may become restructured, creating a series of hierarchical stages. Cognition and rationality are central to morality and the role of affect is minimal. The motivation for morality is a need for acceptance, competence, self-esteem, or self realization (Kohlberg, 1976). Kohlberg's cognitive starting point implies that the structuring of information, the exchange of social perspectives, role taking opportunities and situations stimulating an internal cognitive conflict are important for development. Though family-interaction may provide opportunities for each of these experiences, it is only one of many social groups that may do so. Thus, in Kohlberg's theory neither discipline, nor the family, is most important for stimulating moral development.

Cognitive development is also central to Piaget's two-stage theory of morality (Piaget, 1965). Piaget stressed topics such as the child's concept of rules, respect for rules, and the child's sense of justice, all of which refer to the rights of persons stemming from considerations of equality, social contract, and reciprocity in human relations (Lickona, 1976). In contrast to Hoffman's theory, Piaget considered parents to be of minor importance in stimulating moral judgment. The child respects the parent's authority and thus need not change perspectives. Piaget presupposed that exchange of perspectives may be crucial for the development of autonomous morality. Such an exchange is hypothesized to take place only with other persons equal in social and developmental level, however. Therefore, parents generally may not be capable of stimulating the child's moral development. According to Piaget the interaction with peers is most important for the development of an autonomous morality. The equality of the relationship gives the child the possibility to experiment and to exchange roles freely.

In contrast to Kohlberg's and Piaget's theory Hoffman (1983, 1984b) attributes a central role in stimulating moral internalization to parents (see section 2.1). Hoffman admitted that interactions among peers in homes where inductions are frequently used may also have a constructive effect (Hoffman, 1983). However, the most critical influences are expected to come from the parents. This difference in theorizing is directly related to the conception of morality used. According to Hoffman a norm refers to a conflict between needs felt within a person. A child who has internalized norms not only experiences hedonistic needs but also experiences the needs of other persons. A norm is the internal motivation to consider the needs of others. A child who has internalized norms has a moral orientation characterized by an independence of external sanctions and guilt experience (Hoffman, 1975a). When internalization does not occur the child has a moral orientation based on fear of external detection and punishment.

Hoffman (1970) used a subjective definition of external sanctions. External sanctions are not an objective feature but in the mind of the actor. A child can behave in accord with a moral standard in situations where detection is unlikely, but this behavior may nevertheless be motivated by irrational fears of authority figures or retribution by ghosts or gods. Thus, according to Hoffman, moral internalization refers to a freedom from subjective concerns about external sanctions.

Hoffman characterized a norm using three components (Hoffman, 1983). First, the person feels an obligation to act in accord with a norm and may feel guilty if he does not. Hoffman called this the affective-motivational component of a norm. Hoffman asserted that affect, especially empathy and sympathy, often motivates moral behavior (Hoffman, 1984a). The activation of a moral norm, however, does not guarantee moral action because the egoistic motive may be more powerful. Moral action is not simply the expression of a moral motive but the attempt to achieve an acceptable balance between one's egoistic and moral motives.

Second, and in addition to this affective-motivational component, moral norms also have a cognitive component that includes one's representation of the consequences of one's actual or anticipated behavior for someone else, one's awareness of prohibitions against acting in ways that may harm others physically or psychologically, and one's judgments about the rightness or wrongness of particular acts and the reasons for these judgments. These cognitions pertain to the shaping and transformation of the affective experience. For example, seeing another person's need can make a child feel sorry for him. When the child realizes that he, himself, may have been the cause of the observed distress (i.e., cognitive component) these feelings may be transformed into feelings of guilt.

The third and final component of moral internalization distinguished by Hoffman, is the autonomous component. Activation of a moral norm must be experienced as deriving autonomously from within the self. That is, the cognitive dimensions of a norm should eventually be taken as one's own idea and the associated affect (usually guilt) and disposition to act in accord with the norm experienced as coming from within the self.

To summarize, Hoffman's moral internalization refers to considering the needs of others and has a cognitive as well as a compelling, obligatory quality that is not based on fear of punishment and should derive from oneself. As argued before, Hoffman hypothesized that the discipline techniques parents choose should influence moral internalization.

3.2   Hoffman's information-processing approach to discipline and moral internalization

Hoffman offered a theory of moral internalization integrating affect and cognition. As we have seen in the preceding section an internalized norm is characterized by an affective, a cognitive and an autonomous component. Parental discipline is hypothesized to have the potential power to accomplish internalization (see section 2.1). Hoffman's theory on the underlying process is based on the conceptualizations of representations of events in memory. While information is given to the child in the discipline encounter, however, the child must

17

pay attention to this information. We will therefore discuss how this necessary condition gets fulfilled (section 3.2.1) and how the relevant information gets processed (section 3.2.2). As will be seen, the schemata resulting from such moral encounters motivate an empathic reaction that, in turn encourages the child to take the needs of others into account in subsequent moral encounters (section 3.2.3).

3.2.1   What happens in the discipline encounter?

In the disciplinary encounter the parent attempts to change the child's behavior. The child has done harm to another person, is going to harm someone, or fails to help another person who needs assistance. It appears as if the child either does not notice or neglects the needs of others, and it is up to the parent, according to Hoffman, to draw the child's attention to this oversight. This is exactly what happens in the discipline encounter (Hoffman, 1983).

Many different reactions may communicate to the child that the parent disapproves of the child's behavior. The parent can give all kinds of punishment, warnings, explanations, statements, suggestions, or demands. A child who only gets punished probably has some idea of having done something wrong and although this may stimulate compliance, it does not necessarily promote internalization. Hoffman's conceptualization of moral internalization, implies consideration of the needs of others. But because young children are hypothesized to be hedonistically oriented from birth and not aware of the needs of others, parents must point out another's needs to the child. Thus, to promote internalization inductive reactions are necessary.

Before a child is able to process information about the environment the child must notice this information. More fundamentally, the child must pay attention to the parent's message. According to Hoffman the discipline strategies employed by parents are usually multidimensional (Hoffman, 1970, 1983). Most disciplinary reactions contain both power assertive and love withdrawing properties. These properties are necessary to get the child to attend to the inductive information that may also be present. Too little arousal may prompt the child to ignore the parent. Too much arousal, produced by fear, anxiety, or resentment, may prevent effective processing of the inductive information and focus the child's attention on the consequences of the action for the self and not the consequences for the other.

Not only power assertion and love withdrawal are arousing. Even an inductive message may contain arousing aspects (e.g., the tone of the parent's voice). Furthermore, a certain amount of arousal presumably derives from the parent-child relation itself and the young child's desire to maintain harmony and a good relation to the parent (Hoffman, 1983). It might be difficult to decide whether or not the child is optimally motivated to listen to the parent. Hoffman suggested the optimal level of arousal for processing information is likely be achieved by merely using inductive strategies (Hoffman, 1983). This is also suggested by Lepper (1983), who explained the relation between discipline and moral internalization from an attributional perspective. According to Lepper techniques of social control that are successful in producing compliance and at the same time subtle enough to prevent the child from viewing such compliance as solely a function of extrinsic controls are most likely to promote internalization. Lepper suggested that inductive discipline is sufficiently powerful to stimulate internalization. Consequently, one may wonder whether the use of power and the withdrawal of love only have negative effects on the process of internalization. According to Hoffman in some instances power assertion will be necessary. For example, when a child is beating up on another child and is very angry, the parent may have to exert some power to stop the child. Afterwards, when things have quieted down, the parent may provide an explanation. In this situation the function of power is to stop the ongoing situation rather than to motivate the child to listen to the explanation. Nevertheless, the arousal level is high because the child was already highly aroused (i.e., fighting) and the parent's intervention may have intensified this. It seems obvious under such circumstances that the inductive information will not be optimally processed. Thus it can be hypothesized that although in some situations the use of power is functional, it still may have a negative influence on the information processing.

In sum, when the parent wants to stimulate the child to internalize norms in a disciplinary encounter, the parent should motivate the child to listen, stimulating an optimal level of arousal, and then present an inductive message. An inductive strategy may contain enough components to trigger an optimal level of arousal. The use of power or love withdrawal only increases the level and probably causes a decline of effective information processing by the child.

3.2.2   The processing of information

As already emphasized, the child must process the information provided in the discipline encounter. That is, internalization of norms is characterized by a cognitive, affective and autonomous component (section 3.1). But what information and what kind of processing is necessary to internalize these norms?

In the preceding section we argued that successful discipline involving explanation to the child of why certain behaviors are right or wrong focuses attention on the behavior and allows the arousal present during the disciplinary encounter to be attributed to the act of transgression rather than to the threat of punishment.

When power assertion and/or love withdrawal predominate the aroused anger and/or anxiety may prevent the child from effectively processing any inductive message (Hoffman, 1983). Hoffman based his thesis on research on attention showing that high emotional arousal generally disrupts cognitive processing in complex tasks. Power assertion and love withdrawal may also arouse a motive to restore freedom. Images of past disciplinary encounters may be associated with anxiety as a result of classical conditioning. Consequently, the anticipation of the deviant act may produce anxiety in children and this may lead to avoidance of the deviant act. Power assertion and love withdrawal may be very effective in restraining a child from behaving in a disapproved way, but when the parent is not present the child may not anticipate the anxiety associated with the parent and may behave according to his or her own needs.

What happens when the inductive component predominates with an optimal level of arousal? Hoffman (1983) distinguished cognitive and affective responses to the inductive message:

1. Cognitive responses.

    The inductive message directs the child's attention to the consequences of the transgression for someone else rather than for the self. As a result the child can make a causal connection between his or her own action and the physical or psychological state of the victim. Induction may also communicate to the child that the child is responsible for the distress of the other person. Furthermore, the parent can give the child information about other aspects of the situation such as norms and expectations about how to behave. The parent can also suggest alternative ways of behaving. This information may be totally new to the child in any given instance or it may be a reminder of something previously known but overlooked. The information contains the cognitive component of a norm. Depending on the particular content of the induction used the child's perspective-taking capacity may also be stimulated by the parent's reaction.

2. Affective responses.

    A second component of a norm is the affective component, which produces the obligatory quality of the norm. Before the parent interferes the child does not attend to the other's needs and emotional state. The inductive message directs the child's attention to another's needs and emotions and this produces an affective response in the child. Hoffman (1984a, 1987) assumed the child has an inborn capacity to react affectively to the affect of another child. For example, when a baby hears another baby crying this results in a distress response. Hoffman called such a distress response an empathic reaction. Inductive discipline focuses the child's attention on the victim of the child's actions and, as a result of perceiving the victim's distress, the child experiences empathic distress.[1]

These two responses, moreover, contribute to the cognitive and affective components of a norm (section 3.1).

---

[1] There is a qualitative difference between this affective reaction and the affective reaction to love withdrawal or power assertion. As already noted, the affective reaction to love withdrawal or power assertion concerns the well-being of the self. The affect that derives from the inductive component concerns the well-being of the victim.

As already noted, the third component of a norm is its autonomous quality. Children's cognitive and affective responses to the parent's inductions should be transformed and encoded into memory. Hoffman (1983) explained the dissociation of affective and cognitive responses from the original discipline encounter in terms of information processing. Discipline techniques focusing on the child's action and its harmful consequences allows parental pressure to be low in salience. The child should therefore notice primarily this information and perhaps forget the external pressures.

Furthermore, Hoffman suggested that language should facilitate memory storage of the appropriate materials. Verbal messages are usually stored in memory by their semantic content. If inductive messages are stored at the semantic level, the contextual aspects (e.g., who gave the inductive message, the exact circumstances, the exact words) should disappear. Thus verbal messages may be more easily stored than many power assertive and love withdrawing components.

Hoffman relied on Tulving's dual-storage theory and a model of memory from Craik. The dual-storage theory presupposes the existence of a semantic and an episodic memory. The semantic memory is concerned with the storage of knowledge and meanings. The episodic memory is concerned with the storage of episodes and events. Semantic memory appears to be more enduring than episodic memory. Information in semantic memory is usually incorporated into a complex structure of concepts and their relationships, which also facilitates information retrieval. Thus, semantic aspects will be remembered better than episodic aspects such as who gave the discipline reaction. The parental image is not semantically related to the inductive content.

According to the model of Craik, there are basically three levels of processing that operate successively. First, there is the simple sensory registration of the stimulus. This is followed by the perceptual level of pattern recognition and matching. Finally, there is a deep, semantic level at which the stimulus is enriched by being associated with past images and cognitive structures. The extent to which a stimulus persists in memory depends on the level at which it is processed. Here again, it is assumed that verbal messages will be more easily stored than situational characteristics at the deep semantic level and that semantic messages may be retained in memory for a relatively long time.

In both memory models semantic aspects are stored independent of situational characteristics. Both explain the storage of the information independent of the external agent who provided the information. As already noted, the third component of internalized norms is the autonomous component, which means that although the source may not be forgotten, the moral norm is nevertheless experienced as emanating from the self. Hoffman (1983) gave two explanations which both may further contribute to this experience as originating from within the self. First, self-attribution theory (see Lepper, 1983) suggests that if the external sources are not perceived, or if they are unclear or invisible, children may attribute their actions and thoughts to themselves. When the children do not know the source of the message they will consider the norm as stemming from

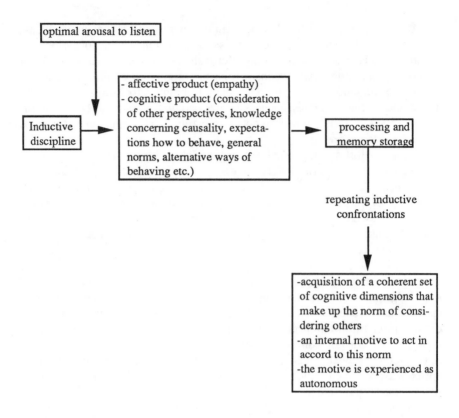

Figure 1   The stimulation of moral internalization

themselves rather than from their parents. Second, the child may perform certain meta-cognitive operations. It is reasonable to expect that this mental activity further loosens the connection between parental image and inductive content. Thus, when asked about the source of the norm, it is assumed that children will attribute their actions and thoughts to themselves (Hoffman, 1983). This reflects the autonomous component of a norm.

The above-mentioned process of how norms become internalized as a consequence of parental discipline is outlined in Figure 1. In a single discipline encounter an inductive message may produce an affective and cognitive reaction within the child, which is then processed and stored in memory. What happens in a single discipline encounter is diagrammed in the (horizontal) upper part of Figure 1. If the parent frequently gives such inductive messages in discipline encounters the child acquires knowledge about how to behave and acquires the capacity to react empathically to a diversity of situations in which another person is involved. The child is motivated to consider the needs of another without feeling urged to do so by any external force. Stated differently, the child has

22

internalized the norm to consider the needs of others (see right (vertical) part of Figure 1).

In summarize, power assertion and love withdrawal may cause fear and anxiety which in turn motivate the child to comply. Classical conditioning may associate certain aspects of the situation, in particular the presence of the parent, with fear and anxiety. Then, although the child does not behave in accordance with his or her own desires, it is unlikely that the needs of others are properly considered. The frequent use of induction, however, increases the likelihood that representations of moral-cognitive structures and feelings associated with these structures are stored together in memory. Because of this semantic storage, moreover, the original source of the norm may disappear and the norm subsequently experienced as autonomous (i.e., internalized). A change in behavior in response to inductive discipline is not a clear instance of compliance in the sense of submitting to someone but rather a change in perspective resulting from the semantic processing of information. Cognitive psychologists originally paid little attention to the influences of affect on cognitive behavior and development. In the 1980's, however, the relationship between affect and cognition has received greater attention (e.g., Arsenio, 1987, 1988; Hoffman, 1986; Radke-Yarrow & Sherman, 1985; Strongman, 1987).

In this section Hoffman's theory of how disciplinary information may be processed was outlined in order to illustrate how norms may be internalized. It seems obvious, however, that the criterion of moral internalization is not just wether or not certain information is stored but also the consideration of another's needs in subsequent moral encounters. In these new situations empathic arousal can be seen as the motive for this consideration (Hoffman, 1982a, 1987). In the following section the relation between empathy and perspective taking, and the relation between empathy and perspective taking with moral internalization will therefore be considered.

3.2.3 The mediating role of empathy and perspective taking in the relationship between discipline and moral internalization

According to Hoffman empathic distress is a motive to consider the needs of others. Consequently empathy plays a central role in his theory of moral internalization. Empathy is closely related to the child's perspective taking. That is, a child may react empathically to another's situation and then wonder where the experienced distress comes from. When the child realizes that the distress stems from another person, the child may then wonder why the other person is distressed. Thus empathic arousal may motivate the child to take the perspective of the other. An empathic reaction may also, however, be the consequence of taking another's perspective (Hoffman, 1987). This reciprocal influence between empathy and perspective taking will be worked out.

23

Hoffman (1987) distinguished five modes in which empathy may be aroused. Some of these arousal modes require rather shallow levels of cognitive processing and are largely involuntary (e.g., sensory registration, mimicry, conditioning and direct associations), while other modes require deeper levels of processing (e.g., putting oneself in other's place). When empathy is aroused the experience of this affective response can be influenced by the child's social-cognitive development. That is, the way in which children experience empathy may depend on their perception of others. Hoffman (1987) called this the "cognitive sense of others". The cognitive sense of others develops and interacts with the affective experience of empathy.

Hoffman (1975b, 1984a, 1987) distinguished four levels in the development of a cognitive sense of others:
a. Self-other fusion. There is no clear separation between the self and the other.
b. Person permanence (at about 12 months of age). The other is a physical entity distinct from self. The child has a stable sense of the separate existence of the other person even when the person is outside the individual's immediate perceptual field, but the child nevertheless tends to attribute to others the characteristics that belong to the self.
c. Perspective taking (at about 2-3 years). The child is aware that the other has independent internal states. The first rudiments of role-taking competence may be present under certain conditions in very young children (even under two years of age). Role-taking competence improves and becomes increasingly complex with age.
d. Personal identity (between 6 and 9 years of age). Others have experiences beyond the immediate situation and their own history and identity as individuals.

According to Hoffman the different levels of social-cognitive development combined with the capacity for affective responding produce the following sequence of the development of empathic distress:
a. Global empathy. Infants may experience empathic distress as a result of automatic, involuntary processes. They have not yet acquired a sense of others as physical entities distinct from the self and therefore the distress cues from the dimly perceived other are confounded with unpleasant feelings aroused in the self.
b. Egocentric empathy. The child may now be aware that another person and not the self is in distress, but the other's internal states remain unknown and may be assumed to be the same as one's own.
c. Empathy for another's feelings. With the onset of role-taking one recognizes that other people's feelings may differ from one's own and are based on their own needs and interpretations of events. Consequently one becomes more responsive to cues about what the other is actually feeling.
d. Empathy for another's life condition. Although one still responds empathically to another's immediate distress, one's empathic response may be

24

intensified or reduced when one realizes the specific circumstances concerning the other person.

Hoffman (1987) also claimed that it is possible that the child's perspective on the situation may change the child's empathic reaction into a related moral affect. When the child realizes that he may be the cause of the victim's distress, empathy may be transformed into feelings of guilt. Similarly, when the child is empathically aroused and cues indicate that someone else caused the victim's distress the child may feel anger at the transgressor or "empathic anger". It is also possible that empathic distress leads to a reciprocal concern for the victim. In this case the child feels compassion or "sympathetic distress" for the victim. According to Hoffman (1984a, 1987), this sympathetic distress arises when the child has a notion of self-other differentiation (second level of cognitive sense of others) and experiences egocentric empathy.

In summary, empathic experiences are influenced by the child's cognitive sense of others and may be transformed into other affects depending on the child's perspective on the situation.

We also argued that empathic distress may be the consequence of the child's perspective taking. According to Hoffman (1984a, 1987) empathy can also be aroused by putting the self in another's place. Perspective taking involves understanding another's thoughts and motives, as well as feelings. A child becomes progressively better able to recognize that the other is in need and to anticipate the consequences of his or her own actions for others. Children with advanced perspective-taking skills can more accurately imagine and anticipate perspectives beyond their own and will also, therefore, experience empathy and related feelings such as sympathy much more often.

It should be clear that empathic arousal and the child's perspective on a situation are closely related. Both can be stimulated by the parent's discipline techniques. When the parent points out the consequences of an action for the victim, the child is stimulated to consider the victim's perspective and may become empathically aroused. Each time the parent gives an inductive message the child may react emphatically and may acquire knowledge about the perspectives of the other people playing a role within the situation. That is, the child's empathic capacity as well as perspective-taking abilities may be stimulated in the long run by such inductive strategies.

What then happens in new moral encounters? Children's cognitive and affective responses to the parent's inductions in early discipline encounters are stored in memory (see section 3.2.2). Hoffman (1983) speculated that these cognitions and affects may later be evoked in moral encounters. Whenever the child is engaged in a new situation an empathic reaction motivates the child to consider the needs of the other. With an increasing perspective-taking ability, moreover, the effects of actions on others can be better comprehended or anticipated and the range of stimuli eliciting empathy may increase. In other words, empathy and perspective taking are both hypothesized to be mediating variables in the relation between inductive strategies and moral internalization.[2] Whenever parents give inductive messages, the child's attention is directed toward another and the child is provided with information about the other. Consequently, the child develops the capacity to react with empathy in a variety of moral encounters and this capacity may in turn motivate the child to consider another's needs.

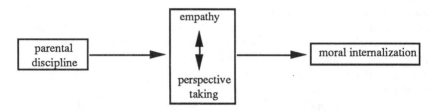

Figure 2   Empathy and perspective taking as mediating variables between parental discipline and moral internalization

In Figure 2 a model of moral internalization is presented. The parent arouses the child to listen by using an inductive discipline strategy. The information provided by the parent stimulates the child to consider the situation (perspective taking) and concurrently stimulates the child's empathic capacity. The feelings of empathy form the basis for subsequent moral decisions. A child who has a good sense of others can respond empathically to the situation, knowing the needs of others and taking them into account in moral decisions. This is what Hoffman called moral internalization. Thus Hoffman stressed an empathy-based morality and in the second part of this research the model presented in Figure 2 will be tested.

---

2   Hoffman suggested that the child's language and social-cognitive skills (e.g. role-taking) influences the moral internalization because the effects of actions on others can be better comprehended or anticipated and the range of stimuli eliciting empathy increases (Hoffman, 1983, 1987). However, language and social cognition are affectively neutral skills that bear more directly on moral competence than on moral motivation. Empathy motivates the child to benefit others. The child feels an internal compulsion to be moral. Empathy is a necessary mediating variable between discipline and moral internalization and, because of the close relationship between empathy and perspective taking, we have decided to consider both variables to mediate between discipline and moral internalization.

3.3   Generalizations from research

The research on child-rearing characteristics and moral internalization have been reviewed several times (e.g., Hoffman, 1963, 1970; Maccoby & Martin, 1983; Rollins & Thomas, 1979; Shaffer & Brody, 1981). Nevertheless it may be useful to summarize the results of these reviews briefly, as will be done in section 3.3.1. Much of this research has been correlational, neglecting the causality problem and the variables that may mediate between parental discipline and moral internalization. One of the exceptions is a study by Janssens and Gerris (in press) who found evidence for the mediating role of empathy in the relationship between discipline and prosocial development. Further evidence for the relationship between empathy and moral internalization and between perspective taking and moral internalization will be presented in section 3.3.2. Finally, some evidence for the existence of a relationship between discipline and empathy and between discipline and perspective taking will be outlined in section 3.3.3.

3.3.1   The relationship between discipline and moral internalization

After reviewing studies on discipline and moral internalization Hoffman (1970) made the following empirical generalization. An advanced moral orientation is associated with the mother's frequent use of inductive discipline and a weak moral development is associated with discipline techniques having high power-assertive components (e.g., physical force, deprivation of material objects or privileges, or the threat of these). Love withdrawal (e.g., ignoring the child, saying that the parent does not like such children) infrequently relates to moral internalization and thus no apparent pattern could be detected.

In the studies reviewed by Hoffman, induction was operationalized in different ways and usually consisted of a broad range of behaviors: Pointing out the consequences of the child's behavior for others, asking the child to account for the behavior, insisting upon reparation, suggesting appropriate alternative actions, and simply telling the child what aspects of the behavior are unacceptable were all classified as induction in the studies reviewed by Hoffman.

The strength and consistency of the empirical relations appeared to depend on the operationalization of moral internalization. Hoffman distinguished two behavioral indicators of moral internalization: Resistance to the temptation to transgress and confession following transgression. These behavioral indicators showed minor correlations with parental discipline. However, two internal state indicators, guilt and moral judgment, showed the most clear-cut pattern of correlation with parental discipline. Most of these results applied to middle-class subjects. Almost no relations are found for lower class subjects. Furthermore Hoffman concluded that, in contrast to the mothers, very few relationships are obtained between father's disciplinary practices and the child's moral development. This was true for boys as well as for girls.

Several years after Hoffman's publication, Rollins and Thomas (1979) also reviewed the studies on parental practices and moral development (operationalized as resistance to temptation, moral judgment, and conscience). Whereas Hoffman found only a few correlations between discipline and moral internalization Rollins and Thomas concluded that power assertion is negatively correlated with moral development and induction positively correlated, irrespective of the operationalization of moral development. Rollins and Thomas did not differentiate between sexes and their conclusions are therefore supposed to hold for boys as well as girls and fathers as well as mothers. Finally, Rollins and Thomas found love withdrawal to be associated with numerous conceptual and/or methodological difficulties. Therefore they did not attempt to generalize about the relation between love withdrawal and moral development.

How can the different conclusions of Hoffman and Rollins and Thomas be explained? First, Hoffman distinguished between several indicators of child morality while Rollins and Thomas did not. Second, Rollins and Thomas did not differentiate between fathers, mothers, sons, and daughters, even though no relation between father's disciplinary style and child moral development was found in the only two studies concerned with this.

A more recent review is that of Shaffer and Brody (1981), although the studies they cited do not greatly differ from the studies Hoffman and Rollins and Thomas cited. All of the studies were published before 1975 and only four of them were published after 1970. It is therefore not surprising that the conclusions are consistent with the conclusions drawn by Hoffman (1970).

The aforementioned reviews found inconsistent relations between love withdrawal and morality. Maccoby and Martin (1983), however, highlighted the possible influence of love withdrawal on moral development. After reviewing several studies they concluded that withdrawal of love may generate anxiety in children and this anxiety may in turn motivate compliance. Compliance does not automatically imply internalization, however. Maccoby and Martin suggested that, at least when used with very young children, love withdrawal may be similar to physical punishment a technique with which parents buy desired behavior. This contrasts with Hoffman's earlier suggestions of love withdrawal having similar effects as induction (Hoffman, 1963).

In summary, the reviews mentioned above indicate that the use of inductive techniques tend to correlate positively with the child's moral development whereas the use of power assertive techniques tend to correlate negatively with the child's moral development. The relationship between love withdrawal and moral internalization is unclear. It seems obvious that this statement is a generalization based on a number of studies. Nevertheless, numerous inconsistencies exist (e.g., findings of no relationship between parental discipline and the child's moral internalization). What may cause these inconsistencies?

Numerous explanations can be offered. First, a possible cause of the discrepant findings is the distribution of scores, which can show considerable variation from study to study. For example, a low to moderate use of power may stimulate the child to behave in a morally acceptable way. Research selecting a low to moderate range of power will therefore produce positive correlations. Severe punishment may not stimulate morality. Research selecting a moderate to severe range of power will therefore produce negative correlations. Studies measuring a broad distribution of scores, moreover, may find no correlation because of a possible curvilinear relation between power and moral internalization (Rollins & Thomas, 1979; Shaffer & Brody, 1981).

Second, interaction effects may exist between parental variables (Rollins & Thomas, 1979). In fact, such an interaction effect can be derived from Hoffman's theory. It can be hypothesized that when power assertion is totally absent no relation may be found between induction and moral internalization because the child is not motivated to listen to the parent. Hoffman (1970) suggested that in reality such a situation may not occur because any discipline encounter generates a certain amount of activation to listen to the parent. When power assertion is low a positive relationship exists between induction and moral internalization. But when power assertion is high, again no relation is expected. This being the case one study might find something different from another study depending on the amount of power assertion used in the sample.

A third possible cause put forward by Shaffer and Brody is that the effect of any disciplinary technique may depend upon the age and the sex of the child to whom it is administered as well as the sex, social class, and other attributes of the parent who administers the discipline.

Fourth, discrepant findings may often be attributed to the imprecise definition and/or measurement of child variables (Shaffer & Brody, 1981). Hoffman (1970), for example, noted that different child variables give discrepant outcomes.

Fifth, and analogous to the above explanation, parental variables can be defined and measured in different ways. Most studies use induction as an undifferentiated category. However, many studies suggest that there are qualitatively different categories of induction (Maccoby & Martin, 1983). Hoffman (1970) concluded that induction is the type of discipline most conducive to moral internalization, but he also suggested that other-oriented induction (i.e., referring to the implications of the child's behavior for other persons) may be of particular importance for moral internalization. Hoffman and Saltzstein (1967) operationalized induction as referring to the consequences of the child's actions for others. They differentiated between a category "induction regarding parent" (e.g., the action has hurt the parent, that an object was valued by the parent) and "induction regarding peers" (e.g., the parent makes reference to and shows concern for the feelings of the victimized child). Induction regarding parents correlated more frequently with the moral indicators than induction regarding victims. In an attempt to explain the development of altruistic behavior, Hoffman (1975c) stressed the importance of pointing out the harmful consequences of the child's behavior for the victim or stimulating the child to imagine the self in the other person's place. These techniques were called victim-centered techniques. Unlike other-oriented induction, these victim-centered techniques also referred to techniques that suggest concrete acts of reparation and techniques that suggest that the child apologize.

Another study from Sims (cited by Keller & Bell, 1979) distinguished between active and passive induction. Active induction, where the child actively takes the other's role, appeared more effective in stimulating altruistic behavior than passive induction (lecturing by the parent). Staub (1979) distinguished between positive and negative induction and hypothesized that positive induction should provide a stronger incentive to act prosocially. Positive induction refers to pointing out the positive consequences of desirable behavior, the increased well-being of other people, and the positive emotions that such behavior induces in the other person. Negative induction is pointing out the negative consequences of the child's undesirable behavior for other people.

Apparently, several types of induction can be distinguished which may or may not bear a relation to the child's moral internalization. The correlation between the use of inductive discipline strategies and the child's moral internalization may also be suppressed when several types of inductive discipline are lumped together. From the studies mentioned above it appears that techniques directing the child's attention to the other person and stimulating the child to be actively involved in the situation may be of particular importance for moral internalization. We will use the term 'victim-oriented discipline' to refer to techniques that direct the child's attention to the other person. In the present study we will distinguish between inductive discipline and victim-oriented discipline and investigate their relationship to the child's moral internalization. Inductive discipline strategies refer to the broad set of explanations or reasons the parent may use to convince the child of the inappropriateness of his or her behavior (see section 2.1). These techniques may not always direct the child's attention to the victim (e.g., "if you keep acting like this you'll lose all your friends"). When the child ignores the victim the child may not become empathically aroused and, as already shown, arousal may be of central importance for moral internalization. Also the child's perspective taking may not be stimulated by inductive techniques. In contrast, victim-oriented discipline may direct the child's attention to the consequences of his or her behavior for someone else rather than for the self (e.g., "look how sad you made him by taking his favorite toy"). This may, indeed, cause empathic arousal. It may also teach the child to refrain from moral transgression by stimulating the child's perspective taking (e.g., "how do you think X would feel if you broke his toy"). And it may teach the child to help another and feel responsible (e.g., "make up to the child for what you did"). As a result, the child can make a causal connection between the own action and the physical or psychological state of the victim. Therefore we hypothesize that victim-oriented discipline relates stronger to moral internalization than global inductive discipline. In addition, we hypothesize that it is important to differentiate not only between inductive discipline techniques but also to operationalize moral internalization in different ways. Furthermore, variables such as the child's sex and age and the parent's sex has to be taken into account.

3.3.2 The relationship between empathy, perspective taking and moral internalization

Our model concentrates on the mediating role of empathy and perspective taking in the relationship between parental discipline strategies and moral internalization. There are some empirical indications that empathy and moral internalization may be related.

In a correlational study, Roe (1980) found a significant positive relation between children's empathy level and consideration of others. Roe also found a positive relation between empathy and children's perception of their parents as fearsome and punitive.

There is more evidence that empathy is a motive for morality (De Veer, Janssens & Gerris, 1988; Eisenberg & Miller, 1987; Feshbach, 1979). De Veer, Janssens and Gerris (1988) have also shown empathy to be positively correlated with cognitive and affective manifestations of moral internalization (i.e., an internal orientation in moral judgment tasks and feelings of guilt). Several times the research on the relation between empathy and morality has been reviewed. In his review, Feshbach (1979) concluded that a negative relation exists between empathy and aggression. Virtually no relations has been found between empathy and social behaviors such as generosity, altruism, cooperation and moral thought. Most research pertains to the relation between empathy and prosocial behavior. In a meta-analytic review Underwood and Moore (1982) also concluded that there is no general relation between empathy and prosocial behavior. They suggested that a reliable association between empathy and altruism develops over time and is found in adults. In their analysis of more than eighty studies published since 1971 Eisenberg and Miller (1987) grouped the studies according to the kind of measures used to assess empathy. Although a relation between empathy and prosocial behavior was found to exist, the degree of association between empathy and prosocial behavior varied depending on the particular measure of empathy. The association between story indices of empathy (presenting hypothetical stories and asking the child's feelings in response to each story) and prosocial behavior, when tested with meta-analytic procedures, was nonsignificant. The association between the other indices of empathy and prosocial behavior, however, were generally positive and significant.

There is thus some evidence that empathy is related to aspects of morality. It should be noted that the reviews of Feshbach, Underwood and Moore, and Eisenberg and Miller primarily concentrate on the role of empathy in the performance of moral actions such as prosocial behavior. That is, empathy may be related to overt behavior. Moral internalization refers to consideration of the needs of others, however. Although moral behavior may be the result of considering the other's needs, it cannot be equated with moral internalization.

In addition to the relationship between empathy and moral internalization the hypothesized relation between perspective-taking ability and moral internalization has been investigated. Perspective taking is often seen as an important prerequisite to moral development (Kohlberg, 1976; Piaget, 1965; Selman, 1976). Perspective taking, then, is considered as a necessary but not sufficient precondition to moral judgment (Kohlberg, 1976; Walker, 1980). Nevertheless, many of the authors who have reviewed the literature concluded that the relation between perspective taking and variables such as prosocial behavior (Iannotti, 1985; Radke-Yarrow, Zahn-Waxler & Chapman, 1983; Shantz, 1975, 1983), moral judgment, and altruism (Kurdek, 1978) is not consistent. Underwood and Moore (1982) used a meta-analytical technique to aggregate over independent studies. In contrast with the above-mentioned reviewers, they concluded that a reliable relationship has to be found between perspective taking and altruism.

It may be concluded that some evidence for an association between empathy and perspective taking, on the one hand, and moral behavior, on the other hand, exists. However, a distinction must be made between moral behavior and moral internalization. As already noted, moral behavior may be a consequence of moral internalization but moral internalization is a broader concept than moral behavior. This means that only limited empirical evidence for the existence of a relationship between the child's empathic capacity and moral internalization and between the child's perspective taking and moral internalization has been found.

3.3.3 The relationship between discipline and the child's empathy and perspective taking

Aside from the hypothesized relationship between empathy and perspective taking on the one hand and moral internalization on the other hand, parental discipline is also hypothesized to relate to empathy and perspective taking. Experimental studies manipulating the level of empathy and measuring subsequent helping behavior provide some evidence for the hypothesis that empathy motivates one to help another. Moreover, a child's empathy has also been shown to be influenced by the instructions used. Trying to imagine how another person feels about the situation arouses more empathy than instructions focussing on the objective information in the situation (Fultz, Batson, Fortenbach, McCarthy & Varney, 1986; Toi & Batson, 1982). Howard and Barnett (1981) encouraged children to focus on the feelings of the less fortunate others. Children in the control group were encouraged to think about the less fortunate others, but without the mention of feelings. Children in the empathy arousal condition were found to show significantly more sad feelings than children in the control condition. These studies indicate that empathy may be aroused by the instructions given by the adult to the child.

There is also evidence for a relationship between perspective taking and disciplinary style. Some studies report the results of a training program of perspective-taking skills. In general, instruction can improve children's perspective-taking ability (e.g., Chandler, 1973; Lowell Krogh, 1985). For example, Bearison and Cassel (1975) studied the effectiveness of verbal communication and differentiated between mothers making person-oriented statements and mothers making position-oriented statements. Person-oriented appeals included regulatory statements that draw attention to the feelings, thoughts, needs, or intentions of the mother, the child, or a third person who may be affected by the child's action. Position-oriented appeals referred to rules or statutes (e.g., "all children have to go to school"). They hypothesized that person-oriented statements would be more effective because they stimulate the child to take the perspective of others. Children whose mothers used person-oriented arguments rather than position-oriented ones were more successful in taking the perspective of another person when required to in a game. Peterson and Skevington (1988) studied the relation between cognitive role-taking and child-rearing method. They distinguished distancing from didactic induction. Distancing typically involves questions that challenge the child's existing point of view, creating a cognitive conflict in the child. Didactic induction typically involves one-way communication strategies that provide logical reasons for the requested behavior change without encouraging the child to discover such reasons himself or spontaneously think about the rationale. Distancing was significantly associated with the child's cognitive role-taking skills, but didactic induction was not related to role-taking skills. This suggests that distancing discipline may influence perspective taking. In other words, it is important to differentiate between the types of information provided by the parent (cf. section 3.3.1).

In summary, evidence has been found for a relationship between the kind of instructions given by an adult and the child's empathic and perspective-taking abilities. Empathy and perspective taking have also been shown to relate to moral internalization. Notwithstanding the fact that the relations between these concepts have been investigated regularly, the mediating role of empathy and perspective-taking ability as an explanation for the relation between disciplinary techniques and moral internalization has not been the focus of much research. In this research, therefore, a model will be tested in which discipline is hypothesized to influence the child's empathy and perspective taking, which are in turn hypothesized to contribute to the child's moral internalization.

To date research focusing on the long-term influences of parental discipline strategies on children's moral internalization is rather scarce. This study concentrates on these long-term influences. In section 2.4 we concluded that a panel study probably would be well-suited to studying long-term effects. The design used in this study is presented in Figure 3. Parental discipline at first measurement occasion (time 1) can be related to the child's moral internalization at the second measurement occasion (time 2). On the other hand the child's moral internalization at first measurement occasion (time 1) can be related to parental discipline at the second measurement occasion (time 2). Comparison of all relations will give us information about the existence of long-term effects.

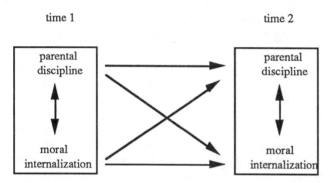

Figure 3   Panel design for studying long-term influences of parental discipline strategies and child's moral internalization

Three main hypotheses will be tested in this study. The first hypothesis bears on the cross-sectional relationships between parental discipline strategies and the child's moral internalization (presented within rectangular forms in Figure 3). In chapter 3 it appeared that Hoffman often mentioned inductive discipline strategies as particularly relevant to the child's moral internalization. Parents who use inductive discipline strategies provide the child with reasons and explanations to motivate the child to change his or her behavior. Hoffman has also stressed the importance of directing the child's attention to the person who is victimized by the child. As a consequence of theoretical as well as empirical research it is suggested in section 3.3.1 that victim-oriented discipline strategies may in particular be related to the child's moral internalization. Therefore, the first hypothesis is:

1. Victim-oriented discipline should relate more strongly to the child's moral internalization than inductive discipline.

The use of a panel model as presented in Figure 3 allows us to test this hypothesis twice: with the data gathered at the first measurement occasion and with the data gathered at the second measurement occasion.

Second, Hoffman presented a persuasive theoretical argument in favor of the dominant effect of parents on children's moral internalization (see chapter 2). His argument rests on the fact that the strength of parental power enables parents to place far greater constraints on the child than the reverse. A second aim in this study, therefore, is to discover whether there is empirical evidence for Hoffman's hypothesis. Consequently, the second hypothesis is:

2. The long-term influence of parental disciplinary strategies on the child's moral internalization is stronger than the long-term influence of the child's moral internalization on the disciplinary strategies the parents choose.

The third hypothesis concerns a further test of Hoffman's theory of moral internalization. In chapter 3 it was shown that the child's empathic capacity and the child's perspective-taking capacity may mediate the influence of parental disciplinary strategies on the child's moral internalization. Thus the third hypothesis is:

3. Parental discipline affects the child's empathic and perspective-taking abilities, which in turn influence the child's moral internalization.

Since the present research focuses on long-term parent-child influences concerning the child's internalization of norms and the parent's discipline strategy, using a cross-lagged panel design, various problems have to be solved. The first problem pertains to the measurement of moral internalization. Moral internalization refers to the motivation to consider the needs of others. How can we assess the extent to which a child is willing to consider the needs of others? Few would disagree that morality lies in action (Blasi, 1980). We can ask ourselves what is left of moral internalization when this is not expressed in the behavior of a person. Moral action is not simply the expression of a moral motive but an attempt to achieve an acceptable balance between one's egoistic and moral motives. The activation of a moral norm, or motive, does not guarantee moral action, because the egoistic motive may be more powerful (Hoffman, 1983). Moreover, the motive for an apparently moral action need not be a moral one. For instance, a child may simply help another in order to please the parent and gain a reward. According to Hoffman's theory this action, no matter how beneficial, would not be moral. Hoffman emphasizes considering the needs of others as characteristic of internalization.

Besides a behavioral manifestation moral internalization also contains a cognitive component, including judgments of what is right and wrong (see section 3.1).

Thus, cognitions are also part of moral internalization. Empirical research indicates a positive relation between maturity of reasoning and moral behavior (Blasi, 1980; Eisenberg, 1982), although Radke-Yarrow, Zahn-Waxler and Chapman (1983) argued that, almost as often, no association have been found.

Furthermore, morality may also be associated with feelings of guilt. Hoffman (1982a) described guilt as the bad feeling one has about oneself when one is aware of having harmed someone else. By pointing out the other's distress to the child, the child is stimulated to consider the perspective of the victim and empathic feelings may be aroused. When the child thinks that (s)he caused the other's distress these empathic feelings are transformed into feelings of guilt. Children who have internalized norms may feel guilty even when they are an innocent bystander. For example, they blame themselves for contributing to the continuation of the other child's distress by not intervening (Hoffman, 1987).

In sum, behavioral, cognitive and affective indicators of moral internalization may exist, and therefore all three components will be studied in order to obtain a conceptualization of moral internalization as adequate as possible.

The second problem pertains to the operationalization of parental discipline. Inductive discipline, and in particular victim-oriented discipline, are hypothesized to motivate the child to consider the other's needs. In the preceding chapter (see section 3.2.1) it was pointed out that power assertion and love withdrawal may influence the effect of induction on the child. Power assertion and love withdrawal can be considered moderator-variables. The aim of these techniques is to arouse the child. This arousal is optimal when the child is motivated to listen to the explanations and reasoning of the parent. The child probably neglects the inductive message when no arousal is achieved (Hoffman, 1983). Thus power assertive or love withdrawing elements have to be present. However, when arousal is too high the child's attention may be directed to his or her own position rather than the inductive message. The central question then is: What is the optimal amount of power assertion and/or love withdrawal to stimulate the child to attend to the inductive message? As already mentioned in section 3.2.1 Lepper (1983) and Hoffman (1983) suggested that inductive messages may themselves contain enough arousal to motivate the child to listen. This leads to the prediction that power or withdrawal of love in combination with induction may divert the child's attention from the inductive message rather than optimalize it. This has consequences for the operationalization of induction. For example, when a parent only uses an inductive message the child is probably motivated to pay attention to the message. But when the parent also uses power-assertion or love-withdrawal the effectiveness of the inductive message decreases. In operationalizing inductive discipline and victim-oriented discipline the degree of power-assertion and love-withdrawal must also, therefore, be considered.

The third problem pertains to the amount of time needed for the parent's disciplinary strategies to show an effect on the child's internalization and vice versa. When we do not take account of time lags properly biased estimates of effects can be obtained (Plewis, 1985). On the one hand the time interval between measures must be long enough to let influences have their long lasting effects. On the other hand, when the time interval is very long, correlations may be too much blurred by other variables influencing discipline and/or moral internalization. For example, it is possible that a change in disciplinary technique takes place early in the measurement interval and that its full effect on moral internalization may have dissipated by the second measurement. As a consequence of not having the optimal time interval the relation may be an under-estimation of the total causal affect of a variable on the other variable. In other words, the temporal lag between repeated measurements may be crucial in a longitudinal study. Gollob and Reichardt (1987), however, argued that it is not necessary to specify the optimal time lag. Although the time lag is important there is no one time lag the only correct one. Effects may be observable with both shorter or longer time lags than the optimal lag. Gollob and Reichardt suggested that the study of many different lags is important to understand causal lags fully. No suggestions in the literature are found pertaining to the best time interval to be taken to guarantee a substantial relation between discipline and moral internalization. In our study we chose the rather arbitrary interval of two years. In 1986 parental discipline and the child's moral internalization were assessed for the first time. Two years later, in 1988, we again assessed parental disci-pline as well as the child's moral internalization.

The final question concerns the age of the children to be studied. It is possible that the influence of parents on children and vice versa depends on the age of the children. That is, parental influence on the children may be stronger with young children than with older children. For this reason we selected several sub-samples of children at different ages. At time 1 we selected second, fourth and sixth grade children. That is, the sample can be divided into three age groups (cohorts), with two years in between each cohort. This design allows us to study changes in moral internalization and parental discipline within each family across a period of two years as well as changes in moral internalization and parental discipline across a period of six years (from 5/6-year-olds to 11/12-year-olds). Before testing the above-mentioned hypotheses, therefore, differences in parental discipline, children's moral internalization, empathic capacity, and perspective-taking capacity will be examined across the different cohorts (see sections 6.1,

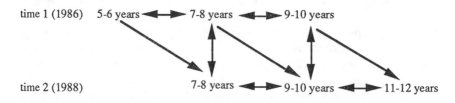

Figure 4   The cross-lagged panel design with two measurements in 1986 (time 1) and 1988 (time 2) and three age groups (cohorts)

6.2, and 6.3). The cohort design is illustrated in Figure 4. In Figure 4 the horizontal arrows represent cross-sectional comparisons. Such cross-sectional comparison can be made with the data from the first measurement occasion (time 1) as well as the data from the second measurement occasion (time 2). The diagonal arrows represent longitudinal comparisons. Each cohort was measured two times, with a two-year interval, which provides measurements of individual change. Finally, by comparing the scores of two independent groups of children at the same age (indicated by the vertical lines in Figure 4), the validity of our measures for a particular age group can also be tested.

5 METHOD

5.1 Subjects

The sample consisted of 150 families with a child attending the second, fourth or sixth grade in one of fourteen elementary schools in the Netherlands at the time of the first measurement. The families were contacted by the teachers of their child. Originally we asked 64 schools to participate in the project. When a school was willing to cooperate a number of randomly selected families were then approached, and 46 % (n = 177) of these families responded positively. The families were visited twice with 22.5 to 24.0 months intervening (M = 23.00). During the first measurement, 177 families participated. When we contacted the families for the second visit 150 families were prepared to participate. Reasons for dropping out were migration (n = 15), family affaires such as divorce (n = 2), or enrollment of the child in a special school (n = 2). Some families simply did not want to participate a second time because they did not have the time (n = 7), and for one family the reason for dropping out was unknown.

The total sample consisted of 150 mothers, 132 fathers, 72 boys and 78 girls. Of the 150 children, at least one parent participated. Background information on the families was collected during the first visit. During this first visit, 47 children attended second grade (cohort 1: 23 boys, 24 girls, M = 5;9 years), 50 children attended fourth grade (cohort 2: 24 boys, 26 girls, M = 7;11 years), and 53 children attended sixth grade (cohort 3: 25 boys, 28 girls, M = 9;10 years). Their position in the family was 5 % only child, 37 % firstborn child, 39 % youngest child, and 19 % middle child.

All the families lived in the neighborhood of Nijmegen, mostly in the country. The mean age of the mothers was 35;6 years (s.d. = 3;9) and of the fathers was 37;8 years (s.d. = 4;1). Most inhabitants of this area are Roman Catholics. In our sample of 150 families, 66 % of the fathers[1] and 71 % of the mothers were religious. During the first visit 93 % of the families were two-parent families, and during the second visit 91 % were two-parent families. Thirty-one percent of the mothers and 95 % of the fathers had jobs outside the house.

The families were classified on the basis of 'ITS beroepenklapper' (Van Westerlaak, Kropman & Collaris, 1975). Three percent of the fathers were classified as unskilled labourers, 21 % skilled labourers, 20 % low-level employees, 9 % self-employed persons, 19 % mid-level employees, and 21 % higher occupations. This classification indicates that there is a underrepresentation of the two lower levels and an overrepresentation of the two top levels.

---

1   Information about the fathers was lacking in 7 % of the cases primarily due to divorce

5.2   Procedure

Each child was individually interviewed at school.[2] The complete interview could be divided into three parts. With the Socio-Moral Interview (S.M.I.) cognitive and affective aspects of moral internalization were assessed as well as the child's level of empathy. The child was then questioned about the relationship between parents and children to assess the child's perspective taking level. Finally, all children were administered the prosocial moral judgment instrument. The interviews were audiotaped and transcribed afterwards.

Parental discipline was assessed by the Discipline Technique Interview (D.T.I.). The parents were interviewed at home, and each parent was interviewed independently of the other parent. During the time that a parent was being interviewed, the other parent filled in questionnaires requesting additional information. All interviews were audiotaped and later transcribed.

Each teacher also filled in a questionnaire concerning an individual child's behavior.

The above-mentioned procedure was followed on the first as well as on the second measurement occasion.

5.3   Measures

5.3.1   Moral internalization

As noted in chapter 4 it is important to consider behavioral, cognitive and affective aspects of moral internalization. Hoffman (1970) distinguished four aspects of internalization appearing in the parent-child research literature. First, the tendency to confess and accept responsibility for one's deviant behavior ('confession'). Second, the amount of resistance to pressure/temptations to behave counter to the standard ('resistance to pressure to deviate'). Confession and resistance to pressure to deviate are, thus, behavioral indicators of moral internalization. The third aspect pertains to the amount of guilt experienced following transgression ('guilt'). And the last aspect refers to the extent to which the child judges moral action independent of any thoughts about sanctions ('internal judgment').

Confession and resistance to pressure to deviate are rated by the child's teacher. The teacher completed a questionnaire concerning the child's behavior in the classroom. The child's guilt and internal judgment is assessed using the Socio-Moral Interview. We did not intend to treat the dimensions of moral internalization a priori as indicators of a single underlying 'moral internalization' concept. It is possible that different aspects of moral internalization begin to

---

[2]   The complete interview took about one hour. For young children, however, this is too long; almost all children were therefore interviewed twice.

develop at different ages and change at different rates. The operationalizations of the four aspects of moral internalization will be described in this section.

Confession

A first measure of moral conduct is the child's tendency to confess and/or accept responsibility for deviant behavior, even when the likelihood of its detection by others is remote. A child who has internalized norms is expected to rectify the situation.

The child's tendency to confess and accept responsibility for one's deviant behavior was rated by the child's teacher. More specifically, the teacher was administered a questionnaire with items describing the child's behavior. The five-item subscale consisted of items referring to the tendency to confess (e.g., "when the child is caught doing something wrong he looks for someone else to blame", "when the child has done something wrong he tries, on his own initiative, to rectify situation"). The items are adopted from Hoffman (1971a). Each item was rated on a six-point scale ranging from never (1) to always (6). Analyses showed one item not to relate well to the other items on the list and after deletion of this item the internal consistency index Cronbach's alpha is .77 at time 1 and .78 at time 2. The final confession score consists of the average for the four remaining items (range 1-6). A low score indicates that the child usually does not confess after wrongdoing and does not accept responsibility. A high score indicates that the child usually confesses after wrongdoing and wants to rectify the situation.

To validate the measurement of the child's tendency to confess and/or accept responsibility for wrongdoing the parents received similar questions about their child's behavior on the second measurement occasion. Confession rated by the teacher on the second measurement occasion is hypothesized to be related to confession rated by the parent. The parent-teacher correlation is found to be positive but not significant (r (135) = .11, p > .05). This brings the validity of this measure into question. When the scale measures a characteristic of the child at least some agreement between parent and teachers has to be found. We may conclude that confession is not validly measured, although a number of alternative explanations for this discrepancy are possible. It is possible that the child's reaction after transgression is mainly determined by the quality of the relation between the child and the adult, by how the adult intervenes after the transgression, and/or how the child expects the adult to react upon transgression. The child's tendency to confess is only manifested after a transgression. Thus, it is suggested that the child's behavior after transgression may also be influenced by the adult who is present in that situation or the immediate reaction of the adult upon the situation. Another possible explanation is that parents and teachers may use different moral standards when judging the child's behavior. For these reasons, no cross-situational consistency of this behavioral aspect has to be found.

Resistance to pressure to deviate

The second behavioral indicator is the amount of resistance the child offers to pressures to behave counter to the standard. Resistance to temptation is usually measured in an experimental situation (Hoffman, 1970), but we used a more indirect, possibly less situation-specific measure. The behavior questionnaire for teachers included three questions about the child's resistance to temptation ("The child can be led into doing unacceptable things", "The child will break a promise when he can benefit from this", "I have to keep an eye on the child and tell him to behave"). These items were rated on a six-point scale ranging from never (6) to always (1). The internal consistency index Cronbach's alpha is .85 at time 1 and .78 at time 2. The child's resistance to deviation was obtained by averaging the ratings of the three items. Thus the minimum possible score equals 1 and the maximum possible score equals 6. High scores correspond to high resistance to pressure to deviate.

At time 2 the parents received similar questions about their child's behavior. As with confession, we related the children's resistance scores as rated by the teacher to the resistance scores rated by the parent to validate the measurement. The parent-teacher correlation is found to be low but significant (r (134) = .35, $p < .001$).

Guilt

Hoffman (1976) viewed guilt arousal as a direct outcome of the harmful effects of wrongful acts on others. When a child responds with empathic distress to the cues of distress from another and the child is also aware of being the cause of another's upset, the child's distress may be called guilt. Guilt arousal, in this view, is a combination of empathic distress and the cognitive awareness of culpability for the other person's distress.
The procedure to assess guilt is adopted from Thompson and Hoffman (1980). Guilt is operationalized as a conscious, self-initiated, and self-critical reaction after wrongdoing (Hoffman & Saltzstein, 1967; Thompson & Hoffman, 1980). In this view guilt is not a purely affective measure but also has a cognitive component.

Guilt was assessed by a semi-structured interview with the children. The Socio-Moral Interview (S.M.I., De Veer, Janssens & Gerris, 1987) consists of four hypothetical stories describing a social situation followed by questions. Each story tells about a child who transgresses a norm. That is, following Hoffman's conception of a norm (see section 3.1), the child in the story does not take the needs of another into account. The protagonist hurts someone, breaks another's toy, cheats, or takes away a child's toy. Stories containing the last two themes were also used by Thompson and Hoffman (1980) to assess guilt. The events in these stories belong to the domain of moral situations classified by Turiel (1978) in that the themes concern the welfare and rights of others and entail the infliction of harm to persons. The stories vary along two aspects. The first aspect refers to the intentions of the transgressor; the transgression is an accident or intended. The second aspect refers to the personal consequences of the act; the consequences are either only personal (e.g., the victim is sad, distressed) or material and personal (e.g., something is damaged or lost and the victim is distressed). Combining these aspects results in four stories. The role of authorities, punishment, laws, rules and formal obligations is minimal. No authority figures are present.

The stories in the S.M.I. also closely parallel those of Chandler and Greenspan (Chandler & Greenspan, 1972; Edelstein, Keller & Wahlen, 1984). All stories have the same composition and consist of seven episodes, with each episode illustrated by a picture.

One of the stories is described below, where the number refers to the episode and a global characterization of the content of the episode is presented. The last column shows the concrete text for one of the four stories. This story refers to an intentional transgression with personal as well as material consequences. The pictures that visualize the text of the story are presented in Appendix A.[3]

1	introduction	The child is playing with his new ball.
2	frustrating event	The ball rolls into the road and a car runs over the ball. The ball is broken.
3	consequences	The child sadly walks away.
4	confrontation with new situation	The child then sees his friend playing with a ball and starts crying.
5	transgression	He then snatches the ball on purpose.
6	consequences for victim	Now his friend doesn't have a ball and starts to cry.
7	introduction of new character	Another boy comes along.

The interviewer reads the story and concurrently presents the pictures. To make sure the child understands the story the child repeats the story. Afterwards, the standardized questions are asked, such as questions concerning the child's reflections about guilt, the child's internal judgment and empathy. Each story is followed by a similar set of questions, and the interviewers are provided with a standardized set of probes for additional information to use when necessary.

The protagonist in each stories is of the same sex and age as the child in question. The stories were presented in random order, and the questions concerning different aspects of moral internalization and empathy were also presented randomly.

The Socio-Moral Interview was too extensive for the 5-6 year-olds, so they received a shorter version consisting of only two stories (the story in which the child breaks another's toy and the story in which the child takes away another's toy).

After each S.M.I.-story the child's guilt reaction to transgression was assessed. The child was stimulated to focus on the child who had committed the

---

3   The pictures are partially based on material used in a study by Gerris (1981).

transgression. Then the child was instructed to assume the role of the wrongdoer. Afterwards the interviewer asked the child to (a) describe how the child would feel after committing the wrongdoing, (b) indicate if the child would feel bad, (c) rate the intensity of that feeling on a seven-point quantitative scale, (d) explain why the child would feel that way, (e) indicate whether the child would feel differently when the act went undetected by others and (f) explain why the child would or would not feel differently. Finally, the child was asked to provide an ending to the story ("What happens next?", "How would you finish the story?").

Three (projected) guilt measures are created on the basis of the child's responses to the questions. The first measure is the intensity of the reported guilt feelings. The other measures are based on the child's explicit expressions of concern for the victim and the quality of the justice principles used to explain the guilt feelings (Thompson & Hoffman, 1980). The guilt measures are scored as follows:

a. Guilt intensity. The child's guilt intensity was assessed in terms of the self-report of the child by means of the quantitative scale used in question (c). When the child felt guilty after wrongdoing, the rating on the quantitative scale reflected the intensity of these guilty feelings. This scale ranges from no guilt to very much guilt. When a child exhibited no guilt at all in response to the wrongful act, a score of 0 was assigned. When the child exhibited the maximum amount of guilt in response to the wrongful act, a score of 6 was assigned. The responses of the child to interview questions (a), (b), and (d) were relevant to determine whether the child's feelings reflected a conscious self-initiated and self-critical reaction. Feelings primarily reflecting feelings of fear to be punished may be seen as self-initiated meaning that these feelings are not evoked by an attendant authority figure. We wanted an indication of the intensity of truly internalized guilt. To prevent our measure of internalized guilt being confounded with external fear, a response reflecting fear of detection was scored as no explicit guilt (score 0). Some children indicated that they would be predominantly happy, that is, in response to question (a) they said they feel happy. These children were also rated as having no explicit guilt (score 0). In other words, higher scores of guilt intensity correspond to more intense feelings of guilt after a transgression.

b. The child's explicit expressions of concern for the victim (in contrast to self concern, such as worry about punishment). The extent to which the child showed concern for the victim was primarily based on the answer to question (d). Concern for the victim was rated on a scale ranging from 0 to 6, adopted from Thompson and Hoffman (1980). Each point of the scale is described. At the low end of the scale, the child does not report feelings of distress or is motivated largely out of self-interested concerns. When a child exhibits no negative feelings (in this case the child often reports feelings of happiness) this is coded in the lowest category (score 0). The child is also scored in one of the lower categories when the child demonstrates distress about the possi-

46

bility of punishment (score 1) or fear of the victim's revenge (score 2). In these cases, there is little or no concern for how the other person actually feels. At the high end of the scale, the child clearly shows a concern for the victim. The child's guilt feelings are linked to the perception of distress in the victim (score 5) and sometimes the child spontaneously assumes the role of the victim and shows that he would be distressed were he or she to be the victim of a similar act (score 6). Some children report feelings of guilt primarily because of behaving badly (i.e., violation of certain standards of conduct). They are not primarily motivated by self-interested concerns but also show little or no concern for the victim. Such responses are coded as an intermediate concern for the victim (score 3 or 4). In this case, the answer on the last question concerning the ending of the story is used to decide to which category the child's answer should be assigned. Only when the transgressor tries to resolve the conflict with the victim is the answer scored as 4. Thus the concern for the victim is rated with a scale ranging from 0 (no concern for victim) to 6 (high concern for victim).

c.   The child's use of justice principles to explain guilt feelings, such as the importance of mutual trust, honesty or personal rights regardless of the external considerations of the wrongful act. This measure was primarily based on the answer to question (f). The use of justice principles was rated on a scale ranging from 0 to 5, adopted from Thompson and Hoffman (1980). The higher the score on this scale, the more the child utilized justice principles to explain guilt feelings. Every category of the rating scale is described. At the low end of the scale, the child simply does not feel guilty (score 0) or is largely concerned with external consequences: fear of detection and punishment (score 1) or fear of the revenge of the victim (score 2). When the act remains undetected, such a child frequently indicates relief as well. At the high end of the scale (scores 4 and 5), the child really feels sorry for the victim independent of possible detection. The principled orientation of the child appears stable. The difference between a 4 and 5, however, is that for a score of 5 the child not only indicates guilt as an outcome of the principled moral orientation but also shows remorse which often leads the child to apologize and attempt reparation, even when the wrongdoing goes undetected. An intermediate level of the use of justice principles (score 3) is assigned when the child reports feelings of guilt and is not afraid of punishment, but wavers (i.e., shows some relief) in undetected transgression.

After some training sessions two independent judges categorized a randomly selected sample of 40 answers. To minimize a halo-effect when categorizing the answers, each guilt measure was scored independently of the other guilt measures. The interrater agreement was 96.3 % for guilt intensity and 88.0 % for both other guilt measures (number of similar codes/total number of codes x 100 %). The answers were binally coded by single person. Guilt intensity, concern for the victim, and use of justice principles were coded separately. This same person also coded the data at time 2, two years later. A sample (n = 40) of the stories at time

1 was randomly selected. The intra-rater reliabilities between the original codes and the codes given two years later were 100 % for guilt intensity, 80.0 % for concern for the victim, and 85.0 % for the use of justice principles.

The ultimate score of each guilt measure is the average of the scores of the stories in the S.M.I.[4] Thus the ultimate scores for guilt intensity and concern for the victim ranged from 0 to 6; the ultimate scores for the use of justice principles range from 0 to 5. To control for whether the scores on the four S.M.I.-stories are interrelated, the internal consistency Cronbach's alpha was calculated for each guilt measure. The internal consistency Cronbach's alpha is found to be .73 for guilt intensity at time 1 and .71 for guilt intensity at time 2. For concern for the victim Cronbach's alpha's are .81 and .73 for respectively time 1 and time 2. Cronbach's alpha's for the use of justice principles are .83 at both measurement occasions.[5]

Table 1   Correlations between 'guilt intensity', 'concern for the victim' and 'use of justice principles' at time 1 (Pearson correlations in upper triangle and correlations with age partialled out in lower triangle)

	guilt intensity	concern for the victim	use of justice principles	age
guilt intensity	...	.75*	.53*	.12
concern for the victim	.74*	...	.62*	.21*
use of justice principles	.55*	.60*	...	.49*

* $p < .05$

---

[4]   At time 1 the youngest children (cohort 1) were administered the short version of the S.M.I.. Differences between cohort 1 and the other cohorts could be due to the differences in the number of stories used. To exclude this possibility the average score of the two stories of the short version is compared to the average score for the other two stories for the children who were administered the complete S.M.I. at time 1 (cohort 2 and cohort 3). All indicators, guilt intensity, concern for victim, and use of justice principles revealed no differences (guilt intensity t (102) = -.22, p > .05; concern for victim, t (102) = .41, p > .05; use of justice principles, t (102) = -.23, p > .05). This corresponds to earlier research, showing no differences of guilt responses across the four S.M.I.-stories (De Veer, Janssens & Gerris, 1987).

[5]   To calculate the internal consistencies Cronbach's alpha for the indicators of guilt at time 1 only cohort 2 and cohort 3 were included in the analyses because the children in cohort 1 were administered only two stories (i.e. the short version of the S.M.I.).

Guilt intensity, concern for the victim, and the use of justice principles are all indicators of guilt. Table 1 shows the correlations between the guilt measures at time 1. The correlations between the guilt measures at time 2 are presented in Table 2. As can be seen, the Pearson correlations among these guilt measures are high. Guilt, as an indicator of moral internalization, is expected to be positively related to the child's age. As can be seen from Tables 1 and 2, most guilt measures are moderately related to age. This shared relation with age increases the Pearson correlations. We, therefore, also calculated correlations with the variance due to age partialled out. As can be seen in Tables 1 and 2, the relations between the guilt measures remain high. This may be due to how they are derived. First, they all derive from the same set of questions. Second, the possible range of a particular guilt measure is partly dependent on the level of another guilt measure. No feelings of guilt in response to interview question (c), for example, also indicates the lowest score on concern for the victim and the use of justice principles. For reasons of economy the data were factor-analyzed and a unidimensional solution is found to be the best characterization of the data. As can be seen in Table 3, the factor loadings for all three indicators are high and the explained

Table 2   Correlations between 'guilt intensity', 'concern for the victim' and 'use of justice principles' at time 2 (Pearson correlations in upper triangle and correlations with age partialled out in lower triangle)

	guilt intensity	concern for the victim	use of justice principles	age
guilt intensity	...	.80*	.60*	.19*
concern for the victim	.80*	...	.64*	.28*
use of justice principles	.55*	.61*	...	.37*

*   p < .05

Table 3   Factor analysis on the three measures of guilt: loadings of two measurement times

	factor loadings	
	time 1	time 2
guilt intensity	.88	.90
concern for the victim	.91	.93
use of justice principles	.81	.82
% variance explained	76%	78%

49

variance sufficient. Furthermore, the factor loadings and explained variance of the data gathered at time 1 and the factor loadings and explained variance of the data gathered at time 2 are almost equal. In subsequent analyses, therefore, the factor score on the factor 'guilt' will be used as an indicator of guilt.

One way of testing the validity of these scores is to examine whether the guilt measure correlates to constructs which are theoretically related to the guilt concept. For example, anticipatory guilt can be expected to motivate resistance to wrongdoing. It may also relate to the antecedents of a positive norm (i.e., consideration of others) (Hoffman, 1976). Therefore guilt is expected to relate to prosocial development. When anticipating the possible consequences for the victim, the child may experience guilt of considering not to help. Children who are primarily self-oriented will experience a fear of punishment following wrongdoing and relief when the act goes undetected. When confronted with a situation in which one has to decide whether or not to help, moreover these children might be expected to reason according to their own needs. When children empathically react to the needs of others, however, they will experience guilt upon seeing the consequences of their behavior and can generally be expected to act more prosocially. In other words, a high guilt level can be expected to correlate with more prosocial reasoning and more prosocial behavior.

To assess prosocial reasoning all children were administered the prosocial moral-judgment instrument (Eisenberg-Berg & Hand, 1979). Two moral dilemmas accompanied by illustrations were used. The central characters are children and the situations are ones that could happen to any child. The first story is about a child playing in a sandbox who views another child being beaten up by a bully and has to decide whether to assist or not. The second story is about a child who is asked to assist another child whose leg is injured, although helping would involve missing a birthday party.

Each story depicts a situation in which the needs of the story protagonist are in conflict with the needs of another child. In each situation, the role of authorities, punishment, laws, rules and formal obligations is minimal. One of the stories is as follows:

> One day while Marcel was playing in his yard, he saw a bully pushing and teasing another child who he did not know. There weren't any grown-ups around. As Marcel watched, the one boy kept pushing the other boy down every time he tried to get back up. Marcel was having a good time playing in his yard, and the bully might pick on him, too, if he tried to help.

After the child has correctly repeated the story, standardized probes are used to ask the child about each story. The order of the stories was randomized. The sex and age of the story characters were matched to the sex and age of the child, and for all stories the child was asked what the story character should do and why he or she should act in the advocated manner. Subsequently, the children were asked what they would do if they were the protagonist and why.

The types of reasoning were coded using categories similar to those employed by Eisenberg-Berg (1979). Three categories refer to victim-oriented prosocial reasoning ('concern for the other's needs', 'overt empathic reaction or role taking', 'internalized affect or norm'). Two categories refer to hedonistic reasoning ("hedonistic reasoning" and "hedonistic pragmatism"). Twenty randomly selected stories were coded by two independent judges, and the interrater agreement is found to be 79 % (number of similar codes/total number of codes x 100 %). Afterwards, all interviews were coded by a single person.

Each child was assigned two scores. The first score indicates the frequency with which the child used the various victim-oriented categories when discussing what the protagonist should do and why. Note that the pros and cons were discussed four times (twice for each story: first for the story character and second for the child himself). Given three victim-oriented categories, and four response opportunities, this score ranges from 0 to 12. The second score indicates the frequency with which the child used hedonistic reasoning categories, and this score may range from 0 to 8. To obtain an overall index for prosocial reasoning, the number of hedonistic categories is subtracted from the number of victim-oriented categories. The overall index may range from -8 to +12 with high scores corresponding to more prosocial reasoning.

Prosocial behavior was assessed using a Dutch version of the Prosocial Behaviour Questionnaire (Weir & Duveen, 1981). The P.B.Q. was created for use by teachers. The questionnaire contains 20 items (e.g., "offers to share erasers or pencils being used in the task", "invites bystanders to join in a game"). Originally, the items were rated on a three-point scale: doesn't apply, applies somewhat or certainly applies. In an attempt to better discriminate between the children, we used a six-point rating scale ranging from never (1) to always (6). Three items showed an uneven distribution of responses, i.e., at least 90 % of the teachers at time 1 and at least 90 % of the teachers at time 2 responded that the item applied to the child (score 4, 5 and 6) or did not apply to the child (score 1, 2 and 3). These items were discarded. The internal consistencies Cronbach's alpha's for the remaining set of 17 items are .90 at time 1 and .91 at time 2. The child's prosocial behavior was taken to be the average of the ratings on these 17 items (range 1-6), and high scores were taken to indicate a strong predisposition to behave prosocially.

The correlations between the guilt scores and prosocial reasoning and prosocial behavior are listed in Table 4. It is possible that some Pearson correlations are spurious due to a relation of both variables with the child's age. Therefore, Table 4 also presents correlations which are controlled for age. Low but significant correlations are found between guilt and prosocial reasoning. However, guilt is only related to prosocial behavior at time 2. Validation of guilt by comparison with prosocial development is weak but satisfactory.

Table 4   The relation between guilt and prosocial reasoning and prosocial behavior (Pearson correlations and partial correlations controlling for the
child's age)

	pearson corr.		partial corr.	
	prosocial reasoning	prosocial behavior	prosocial reasoning	prosocial behavior
guilt				
T=1	.36*	.10	.27*	.14
T=2	.24*	.28*	.17*	.30*

*   p < .05

Internal judgment
Hoffman (1970) distinguished between two different types of moral orientation. Children whose conduct is controlled by the anticipation of rewards for
acceptable behaviors and punishment for unacceptable behaviors are said to have
an external moral orientation. They reflect an orientation toward obedience and
punishment. On the other hand, children who behave in accordance with their
own standards even when authority figures are not present to approve or praise-
worthy conduct or to punish transgressions are said to have an internal moral
orientation. They show conscience as a directing agent or a principled orientation
and show interest the other's needs.
    The children were asked to make moral judgments about four transgressions,
incorporated into the S.M.I.-stories. The purpose of this question is to determine
what children think about moral issues and the extent to which their moral
reasoning is independent of external sanctions. Assessments were made of the
children's justifications for their evaluation of courses of action as right or
wrong. We asked: "Can you take away a child's toy? Why or why not?; Can you
hurt somebody? Why or why not?; Can you cheat in a game? Why or why not?;
Can you break another's toy? Why or why not?"
    In a pilot study (De Veer, Janssens & Gerris, 1987) all of the arguments put
forth by the children were listed. The arguments were found to fall into six different categories: (1) Appeal to authority. The authority, typically a parent, pro-
hibits the act. The act is wrong because it is counter to the wishes of the parent
and/or transgressions will be punished. (2) Appeal to the interpersonal relationship between children. You better not do it because the victim will take revenge
or will end the friendship. (3) The act is wrong because it harms another. The
child refers to the welfare of others. (4) When you commit such an act you will
be upset and distressed and you will feel guilty. (5) The act is wrong, you simply
should not do it. (6) You should not do that because it is not kind, it is not fair.
The child labels the act.

Every answer could be coded in at most two categories. Some children contented themselves merely by stating the violated rule (category 5) or affirming their evaluation (category 6) and then went on to give a rationale. To count such initial statements, however, seemed to distort the frequency data. Nominal-evaluative statements were counted, therefore, only when they were the only response provided by the child. For each story the child's response was coded as external (score 0, categories 1 and 2, e.g., "you will be punished for that", "the child will get back at you") or internal (score 1, categories 3 through 6, e.g., "the other child does not like that", "I would feel guilty", "you are not allowed to do such things", "it is unfair"). When several arguments were offered the most internal argument was taken. Two independent judges coded a randomly selected sub-sample of 40 stories. The interrater agreement is 88.0 % (number of similar codes/total number of codes x 100 %). The remaining answers were coded by a single individual. This person also coded the data of time 2, two years later. A sample (n = 40 stories) of the answers at time 1 was randomly selected. The intra-rater agreement between the original codes and the codes given two years later is 86.7 %.

The internal consistency Cronbach's alpha's of the scores for the four S.M.I.-stories are .45 at time 1 and .46 at time 2.[6] The relation between the scores for the four stories is found to be rather low. The final score is the average of the scores for each story.[7] Because the answers are scored as either external (score 0) or internal (score 1) the internal judgment score also ranges between 0 and 1.

The validity of this measure was checked by comparing the data with data from other research. Hoffman and Saltzstein (1967) did not examine age-related changes or distributions of scores, nor did Hoffman in his 1970 review. Others (see Turiel, 1983) have investigated the justifications children use in judging different social situations. In these investigations most children are found to consider the moral transgressions wrong simply because these acts harm or deprive others (this corresponds with category 3 in the present research). The argument that the act is always wrong was also found to be frequently used (this corresponds with category 5 in the present research) (see Nucci, 1981). Davidson,

---

6   To calculate the internal consistency Cronbach's alpha of the indicator of internal judgment at time 1 only cohorts 2 and 3 were included because the children in cohort 1 were administered only two stories (i.e. the short version of the S.M.I.).

7   At time 1 the youngest children (cohort 1) were administered the short version of the S.M.I.. Differences between cohort 1 and the other cohorts could therefore be due to the differences in the number of stories used. To exclude this possibility the average score for the two stories in the short version is compared to the average score of the other two stories from the children who were administered the complete S.M.I. at time 1 (cohort 2 and cohort 3). There were no differences (t (96) = .65, p > .05). This corresponds with earlier research showing no differences in guilt responses for the four S.M.I.-stories (De Veer, Janssens & Gerris, 1987).

Table 5 Distribution of different justification categories used by different age groups for familiar moral transgressions (see Davidson, Turiel & Black, 1983, Table 7, p. 60)

Category	6-year-olds n=80a	8-year-olds n=72	10-year-olds n=88
appeal to authority or punishment avoidance	36%	17%	14%
others' welfare	60%	61%	47%
appeal to fairness or obligation	4%	20%	33%
other categories	0%	2%	6%
total	100%	100%	100%

a n = total number of responses per column

Turiel and Black (1983) asked six-year-olds, eight-year-olds, and ten-year-olds to judge transgressions and they found a comparable use of justification categories for familiar moral transgressions. Their coding scheme differs slightly from the coding scheme used in the present research because their coding scheme also includes justifications of conventional transgressions (e.g., "a girl should greet her friends by bowing rather than by the customary greeting"). The main categories used in the Davidson et al. study to justify familiar moral transgressions are "appeal to authority", "punishment avoidance" (including social condemnation), "others' welfare", "appeal to fairness", and "obligation". When certain categories are collapsed, however, the two systems are quite comparable. Table 5 shows the frequency of categories mentioned by the different age groups in the Davidson et al. study. The answers given in our study, categorized according to the system of Davidson et al., are presented in Table 6. A comparison of Tables 5 and 6 shows that the distribution of answers within each age group and across age groups are very similar. Most answers refer to the others' welfare and the usage of this argument tends to decrease with age. References to authority and punishment (categories 1 and 2) also appear to decrease with age, while references to feelings of obligation, norms, and fairness (categories 4, 5 and 6) appear to increase with age. This correspondence suggests that our assessment of internal moral judgment capacities is a valid one.

The primary purpose of the judgments we elicited was to get an indication of the internal basis for the children's judgments. Following Hoffman's formulation of moral internalization it can be hypothesized that younger children are externally oriented because they are only aware of their own hedonistic needs.

Table 6   Distribution of different justification categories in the moral judgments of different age groups in the present research

		age of children			
Category	number of category	5/6-years[a] n=104[b]	7/8-years n=422	9/10-years n=464	11/12-years n=219
appeal to authority or afraid for revenge	1+2	32%	21%	17%	9%
others' welfare	3	56%	57%	52%	47%
appeal to fairness or obligation	4+5+6	13%	23%	31%	44%
total		100%	100%	100%	100%

a   5/6-year olds are cohort 1 at time 1
    7/8-year olds are cohort 2 at time 1 and cohort 1 at time 2
    9/10-year olds are cohort 3 at time 1 and cohort 2 at time 2
    11/12-year olds are cohort 3 at time 2
b   n = total number of responses per column

Table 7   Distribution of internal judgment scores at time 1 and time 2

	mean score	time 1	time 2
external	$\leq .25$	5%	1%
predominantly external	$> .25$ and $\leq .50$	12%	7%
predominantly internal	$> .50$ and $\leq .75$	20%	14%
internal	$> .75$	63%	78%
Total		100%	100%

Socialization experiences, thus, might stimulate the child to become more internally oriented. At time 1 the number of internal judgments is only weakly associated with the age of the child (r (148) = .19, $p < .05$). Moreover, an age-related shift towards a more internal basis of evaluation is not found at time 2 (r (150) = .13, $p > .05$). This lack of a finding is probably due to a ceiling effect. As can be seen in Table 7 the children are divided into four categories depending on their internal judgment scores. The categories are: external, predominantly external, predominantly internal, and internal. For example, a child is categorized as external when the ultimate score is less than or equal to .25. The percentages of children within each category are presented in Table 7. As shown in Table 7 most children gave internal or predominantly internal judgments. At time 2 a very few children gave external judgments. Eight percent of the children had a score that could be labeled as external or predominantly external. This puts doubts on the usefulness of this indicator to adequately differentiate between the moral internalization of the children in the sample of this study. The indicator internal judgment will therefore be excluded from further analyses.

5.3.2   Empathy

To assess the child's tendency to respond empathically we looked for emotional responses based on another's emotional state. We also considered whether the child's emotional responses were combined with feelings of sorrow or concern for another's welfare. Empathy is operationalized as a situationally responsive measure having an affective as well as a cognitive component. Every S.M.I.-story ends with the introduction of a new character. This new character passes by after the transgression. In order to assess the child's empathic level the children were stimulated to take the role of this passer-by and were asked how they would feel if they saw the transgressor and the victim. In this assessment the interviewer presented a card with five faces illustrating five different emotional reactions. Four faces expressed four different emotions, either anger, sadness, fear or happiness and one face was neutral ("just OK"). The child was asked to choose the emotion that most resembled the child's own emotion when seeing the children from the perspective of the passer-by. The interviewer then asked the child to motivate this choice ("Why do you feel that way?"). Answers were scored as empathic (score 1) when the child reacted affectively and also expressed a concern for the victim. For example, children who felt sad because they saw the victim crying and felt sorry for the victim were scored as giving an empathic response.

During the interviews it appeared that the child's reaction was related with the child's perspective-taking ability. Older children knew that the figure passing by had not seen what had happened. They were able to differentiate between their information and the information available to the passer-by. They often responded to feel just OK because the passer-by could not know what had happened. Younger children could not correctly take the role of the other character and thus assumed that the figure passing by knew exactly what had happened and why the child was crying. These children often felt empathy for the victim or were angry with the transgressor. That is, these children were more likely to have an empathic reaction than the older children simply because they did not differentiate correctly between the perspectives of different characters. In other words, this measure of empathy does not appear to be a valid one and will therefore be excluded from any further analyses.

At the time of the second assessment, two years later, we controlled for the confounding between perspective taking and empathy. In this assessment we asked children how they would feel if they did not know what had happened. In addition, we also asked the children how they would feel if they did know what had happened before. Children who felt sad and referred to the victim ("I was sad because I feel sorry for him") showed an empathic reaction (score 1). When a child knows the reasons for the victim's distress empathic feelings of sadness can easily be transformed into feelings of anger and this was also scored as 1 (Hoffman, 1982b, 1987). Children may feel angry with the transgressor because of his or her behavior toward the victim. Such responses were therefore coded as empathic because the children affectively reacted to the emotion of another and also referred to the situation of the other person. As seen in section 3.2.3 vicariously induced empathic arousal may produce sympathetic concern for the other and/or aversive arousal (anger with the transgressor) by cognitive mediation. Hoffman (1987) called these emotions sympathetic distress and empathic anger. In this study we measured both of these empathy-based moral affects. Affective reactions which could not be motivated by the child or are based on egocentric reasons (e.g., "Maybe that annoying child will start teasing me as well!") were also scored as nonempathic (score 0).

As just mentioned each S.M.I.-story was evaluated twice by each child in the second assessment: when the figure passing supposedly did not know what had happened and when the figure passing supposedly knew what had happened). Empathy is scored as the total number of empathic responses (with a maximum number of eight) divided by the total number of responses. Thus the ultimate empathy score is the proportion of empathic responses. Therefore a minimum empathy score of 0 and a maximum empathy score of 1 could be obtained for each child. The relation between the eight responses is reflected by an internal consistency index Cronbach's alpha of .72.

At the second measurement occasion we also asked parents and teachers to rate the child's tendency to react empathically. The scale consisted of eight items, selected from Bryant's Empathy Scale (Bryant, 1982). This scale is a self-report measure of emotional empathy designed for children. The eleven positive statements formed the basis for our questionnaire. Six items intended to differentiate between cross-sex empathy and same-sex empathy were collapsed into three sex-neutral statements. Because adults were asked to rate the child's empathy the remaining eight items were reformulated (e.g., "It makes him/her sad to see a child who can't find anyone to play with.", "He/she really likes to watch people open presents, even when he/she doesn't get a present him/herself."). The adults were asked to respond to each item on a six-point scale ranging from never (1) to always (6). The eight items constitute a reliable scale (Cronbach's alpha for the teachers is .72, Cronbach's alpha for the parents is also .72). The child's empathy score on our task correlates with the teacher's rating of the child's empathy (r (137) = .23, $p < .05$, with age partialled out because of possible artificial relations that may occur when both variables are related to age) and the parent's rating of the child's empathy (r (136) = .17, $p < .05$, with age partialled out). These correlations suggest that we have a valid measure of empathy. Given the different foci of these measures, the first being context-specific and the latter being more global, these positive correlations provide some confirmation for the view that they are assessing the same empathy construct.

5.3.3   Perspective taking

Selman (1976) has formulated a general developmental sequence of perspective taking. In his model, he describes five stages of social-cognitive understanding spanning the period from childhood to adolescence. Development of social-cognitive understanding is operationalized by Selman as a progressive increase in the number of elements and relations that must be kept in mind (Higgins, 1981). Each stage represents a cognitive structure used by the child to define and resolve issues of social interaction. The first level distinguished by Selman (1976) is the level of egocentric perspective taking. A child at stage 0 (about 4 to 6-year-olds) is unable to differentiate between different points of view. About 6 to 8-years-old children realize that people feel or think differently because they are in different situations or have access to different information. This is the stage of subjective or differentiated perspective taking (stage 1). At stage 2, children are able to reflect on the self's behavior as seen from the other's point of view (self-reflective or reciprocal perspective taking, about ages 8 to 10). However, these reflections do not occur simultaneously. Only at stage 3, when the child is able to view the two-person situation from a third-person perspective does the child exhibit third person or mutual perspective taking. This stage 3 reasoning is typically shown by 10 to 12-year-olds. Finally, the highest level in Selman's stages of perspective taking is stage 4, which consists of social and conventional system perspective taking. That is, the perspective taking is raised from the level of the dyad to the level of the general social system and the child realizes that each self considers the view of the social system.

Selman distinguished several domains in which the child's level of perspective taking may be manifested, such as close friendships, peer group organization and parent-child relations. In the present research we confined ourselves to the domain of parent-child relations and several questions about the parent-child relationship were asked. The questions referred to four characteristic issues of the parent-child relationship: the function and rationale for punishment (e.g., "Why do parents sometimes punish their children?", "Do you think that children should be punished when they disobey?", "How does punishment work, what does it do for children?"), demands for obedience (e.g., "Should children always obey their parents?", "Why do parents want their children to obey them?"), factors that cause conflicts (e.g., "Parents and children sometimes do not get along, how can this happen?"), and methods parents and children employ for conflict resolution (e.g., " How can you best end a disagreement?"). The interview relied on a standard set of questions. The interviewers were also trained on the stages of perspective taking development and encouraged to ask additional questions when unsure of the child's level of reasoning about a particular issue.

The child's perspective on every issue was scored according to the system developed by Bruss-Saunders in Selman (1979). This coding system does not differentiate between the last two stages (stage 3 and 4). At the lowest level (stage 0) the child has egocentric and pragmatic conceptions of the parent-child relationship. The child can label other's overt feelings but does not see the cause and effect relation between social actions. Stage 1 conceptions are characterized by an identification with parental views. The child is aware that the parent has his or her own perspective which may or may not be similar to the child's perspective. However, the child tends to focus on the perspective of the parent. The main characteristic of stage 2 conceptions is a rather strong focus on the quality of the emotional ties between parent and child. The children can anticipate other's perspectives on their own psychological state and realize that this anticipation influences their perspective on others. A child showing stage 2 reasoning can form a coordinate chain of perspectives but cannot yet abstract from this process. At the highest level coded in this study (stage 3) the parent-child relationship is considered to be both a reflection of and an influence on the parent's and the child's personality functioning. The child can step outside the two-person dyad and view the interaction from a third-person perspective.

Each of the four topics was coded independently. That is, all protocols were first considered for the level of perspective taking for the function and rationale for punishment. Subsequently, the child's perspective of demands for obedience was considered, etcetera. The following procedure was used in scoring the child's responses to each issue. To assign scores to the children's responses two judges were made familiar with the above mentioned stages. Then the part of the interview concerning one of the four issues was read to evaluate the child's overall level of thinking and when the child clearly showed one level of thinking this level was assigned. When a child continuously showed stage 1 reasoning, for example, a score of 1 was assigned. Sometimes a child exhibited two levels of reasoning. In this case the judge had to decide which level was dominant. When one stage dominated the answer was scored as a major/minor stage (e.g., 2(3) = major stage 2 and minor stage 3, 3(2) = minor stage 2 and major stage 3). When no level clearly dominated the answer was assigned an intermediate score (e.g., 1-2 = stage 1 as well as stage 2). Two judges coded all of the answers in the sample independently (300 protocols, 150 protocols at each measurement occasion). Inter-rater agreements were 79% for function and rationale for punishment, 78% for demands for obedience, 79% for causes of conflicts, and 83% for resolutions of conflicts. Protocols on which the two coders did not agree were discussed. Finally, there was an overall agreement about the scores. To compute an average issue score for all four issues we transformed the scores into the following numerical equivalents: $0 = 0$, $0(1) = 0.33$, $0-1 = 0.5$, $1(0) = 0.67$, $1 = 1$, $1(2) = 1.33$, $1-2 = 1.5$, $2(1) = 1.67$, $2 = 2$, $2(3) = 2.33$, $2-3 = 2.5$, $3(2) = 2.67$ and $3 = 3$ (see also Selman, 1979, p. 350). These numerical equivalents of the four scored issues are then added together and divided by four. That is, the children's perspective taking scores could vary between 0 and 3. The internal consistency Cronbach's alpha's for the four issues are .68 at time 1 and .73 at time 2.

5.3.4   Parental discipline

To get an idea of how the parents in this study disciplined their children, each parent was interviewed. In the Discipline Technique Interview (D.T.I.) the parent was confronted with eight hypothetical situations in which his or her child transgressed a norm. The stories describe situations where the child does something to someone else. Thus all situations contain a moral norm. Such situations may lead to a disciplinary encounter (see section 2.1). This means, according to Hoffman, that the parent attempts to change the child's behavior. Because situational characteristics, such as intention of the child, the consequences of the transgression and whether the victim is a child or an adult, influence the parental disciplinary reaction (Grusec & Kuczynski, 1980; Janssens, Janssen, Bernaerts & Gerris, 1985) the situations leading to discipline vary along three dimensions: The intention with which the child acted (on purpose versus accidental), the consequences of the child's action (personal versus personal and material), and whether something frustrating has happened to the child prior to transgression. Considered together, these three dichotomies resulted in eight different stories (see Table 8). The victim is always a child. In the case of something frustrating happening to the child prior to transgression, the stories are identical to those used in the S.M.I. (see Table 8, story numbers 1, 2, 3 and 4). The eight situations were presented to the parents in random order.

Table 8   Situations in the Discipline Technique Interview

no.	short description of the act	frustrating event before transgression?	are the consequences intended?	kind of damage[a]
1	hurting someone	yes	no	p
2	breaking someone's toy	yes	no	p+m
3	cheating in a game	yes	yes	p
4	snatching someone's toy	yes	yes	p+m
5	hurting someone	no	no	p
6	tearing another's clothes	no	no	p+m
7	making fun of a classmate	no	yes	p
8	tearing up someone's favorite poster	no	yes	p+m

a   p = personal damage (distress)
     m = material damage

60

The interviewer reads the story and asks whether the parent understands the story. Then the interviewer asks "Would you do or say something?". When the parent responds yes, the interviewer then asks "What would you do or say?". The interviewers are provided with standardized probes for additional techniques or for more detailed information whenever the parent uses vague terms such as "I would explain" or "I would scold".

All reactions of the parent to each hypothetical situation are coded with a modified version of the coding system used by Grusec and Kuczynski (1980). The coding system lists 25 disciplinary reactions, such as physical punishment, deprivation of material objects or privileges, ignoring the child, disapproval of the child's behavior, suggesting alternative ways of behaving, referring to the consequences of the child's action for the victim, and stimulating the child to repair the damage.[8] There was 81.5 % agreement between two independent judges in the categorization of responses for eight randomly selected interview protocols (64 situations).

Inductive discipline is defined as techniques in which the parent tries to motivate the child to change his or her behavior by explaining. Inductive categories are pointing out the material or personal consequences of the act for the child him- or herself or for the victim, stimulating the child to take the role of the victim, and all other forms of explanation.[9] For each situation the number of inductive codes was calculated. The internal consistency Cronbach's alpha across the eight different situations is found to be .57 at both measurement points.

Victim-oriented discipline is defined as the frequency with which the child's attention was drawn to the consequences of the child's action for the victim. The victim-oriented categories are pointing out the material or personal consequences for the victim, stimulating the child to repair the damage or restore the relation-

---

[8] Labels for the list of disciplinary categories: 1. physical punishment, 2. threatening with physical punishment, 3. nonphysical punishment, 4. threatening with nonphysical punishment, 5. isolating, 6. threatening with isolation, 7. time-out to calm down or think the matter over, 8. physical intervention, 9. nonphysical intervention, 10. ignore the child, 11. command to do something instantly, 12. disapprove of the child's behavior, 13. stimulating to restore the relationship with the victim, request to apologize, 14. request to repair the damage, 15. demand alternative future behavior, 16. point out the material consequences of the act for the victim, 17. point out the personal consequences of the act for the victim, 18. point out the material consequences of the act for the child as a transgressor, 19. point out the personal consequences of the act for the child as a transgressor, 20. stimulate the child to take the role of the victim, 21. point out that the child him- or herself would not like that either, 22. point out that the victim would not act to the child in such way either (reciprocity), 23. give further information/explanation, 24. explanations which contain no new information, 25. say that the child has to solve the situation by him- or herself.

[9] Inductive discipline categories are categories 16 through 24 (for description see preceding note).

61

ship with the victim, and stimulating the child to take the role of the victim.[10] The internal consistencies Cronbach's alpha across the eight situations are .48 at time 1 and .54 at time 2.

Although the interview mainly consisted of standardized questions and standardized probes some parents tended to provide detailed descriptions while other parents remained fairly global. Moreover, some parents reported using punishment much more often than other parents. As already noted, punishment may distract the child's attention from the information being provided by the parent (see also chapter 3). To control for these effects the overall score is divided by the total number of reactions given by the parent. The final inductive discipline score is the total number of inductive codes divided by the total number of reactions. Similarly, the final victim-oriented discipline score is the total number of victim-oriented codes divided by the total number of reactions. That is, the parent's score on inductive discipline reflects the proportion of inductive reactions present in the total number of parental reactions. The parent's score on victim-oriented discipline reflects the proportion of victim-oriented reactions present in the total number of parental reactions. Because both scores are proportions the scores can range from 0 to 1.

The low internal consistencies may have been a product of the choice of situations. As already noted the choice of a disciplinary strategy is determined at least in part by situational characteristics. Put differently, the D.T.I. is intended to obtain an overall impression of the parent's disciplinary style and thus involves a variety of situations. This variety, however, may also suppress the degree of internal consistency. The finding of some internal consistency across different situations nevertheless suggests some coherence in parental disciplinary styles and that this variable can be treated as a cross-situational trait. Furthermore, if the choice of parental discipline strategy is completely triggered by situational characteristics we would expect only minor differences between parents when confronted with the same set of situations. As can be seen in Table 9 parents clearly differ in the amount of inductive discipline and victim-oriented discipline. This also fits with the impression of the interviewers who visited the parents.

We tried to get more evidence for the existence of a global disciplinary style, despite situational influences. More stable characteristics are expected to relate to disciplinary style as measured by the interview. One such characteristic is the sex of the parent. As can be seen in Table 10 mothers tended to use significantly more inductive discipline and more victim-oriented discipline than fathers. This difference is replicated in the second measurement point. This seems to fit with findings of Janssens and Gerris (1988) who tested a model to explain parental discipline. Part of the model concerned the hypothesis that discipline is a consequence of how the parent thinks about childrearing. In their research, they found

---

[10] Victim-oriented categories are categories 13, 14, 16, 17 and 20.

Table 9   The distribution of inductive and victim-oriented discipline by mothers and fathers

| | inductive discipline | | | | victim-oriented discipline | | | |
| | time 1 | | time 2 | | time 1 | | time 2 | |
proportion	mother	father	mother	father	mother	father	mother	father
≤ .10	18%	34%	19%	40%	13%	20%	7%	20%
.11-.20	32%	38%	31%	31%	35%	41%	35%	39%
.21-.30	33%	18%	32%	21%	33%	32%	35%	28%
.31-.40	15%	10%	17%	6%	17%	5%	17%	12%
>.40	2%	0%	1%	2%	2%	2%	6%	2%

Table 10 Differences between mothers and fathers in the proportion of inductive discipline and victim-oriented discipline

| | mothers | | fathers | | | | |
	mean	st. dev.	mean	st.dev.	t-value	d.f.	p
inductive discipline							
T=1	.20	.10	.15	.10	4.91	131	p < .001
T=2	.20	.10	.15	.11	3.83	130	p < .001
victim-oriented discipline							
T=1	.21	.10	.18	.09	3.57	131	p < .001
T=2	.23	.10	.19	.10	3.71	130	p < .001

that parents who focus more upon conformity in childrearing also tend to use more power assertion. In other words, situational factors may always play a role in parental discipline but there is also evidence for a general parental disciplinary style.

To indirectly validate the data gathered in the D.T.I. the interviewers were asked to rate the amount of inductive discipline the parents used after the second measurement. This is a more subjective and intuitive judgment concerning parental inductive discipline. The interviewers were asked to consider all information available during the visit. The ratings were predominantly based on information obtained from the parent. Mostly the child was not present during the visit, so parent-child interactions could not be observed. Inductive discipline strategies were defined as strategies used by the parent to influence the child's behavior by giving information, explaining. The interviewers rated on a five-point scale. Interviewers were trained prior to data collection. Measures of interrater-agreement were established by computing the percentage of agreement among the scores of two raters for 17 videotapes where the parent interacts with the child, who is trying to solve a puzzle (Wiggly Block).[11] Agreement was defined as the occurrence of scores which differed by no more than one point (see also Jay & Farran, 1981; Russell & Russell, 1989; Ten Haaf & Janssens, in press). The mean percent of agreement between two raters was 86 % (range 77 % - 100 %). The correlations between the ratings of the interviewers and the degree of inductive discipline assessed during the interview are moderately high in magnitude (for mothers r (149) = .29, p < .05; for fathers r (129) = .58, p < .05). This indicates that there is an association between the more subjective, intuitive judgment of the interviewer and the parental use of inductive discipline.

There is some other research on the relation between parental discipline assessed through self-report (e.g., an interview) and another person's perceptions of parental discipline. In a study by Brook, Whiteman, Gordon, Brenden and Jinishian (1980) a substantial correspondence was found to occur between maternal self-reports and adolescent reports of maternal behavior. Nevius (1984) also found a significant correlation in the lower-class sample between mothers' and 10-years-old sons' perceptions of the mothers' inductive discipline strategies. This correlation disappeared with a middle-class sample, however. Such correspondence between the parent's and the child's perceptions may indicate that parental self-report data give an indication of the parent's behavior in real-life situations.

Another question concerning the predictive value of parental self-reports in an interview concerns the relation between self-report through an interview and actual child-rearing behaviors. Ten Haaf and Janssens (in press) studied the relation between measures of inductive discipline obtained by using different assessment methods. They also assessed the parent's use of inductive discipline strategies with the same type of interview as the D.T.I. In this interview parents were confronted with a hypothetical situation and asked how they would react. Ten Haaf and Janssens also observed the parent-child interaction. Observations were carried out in two different types of situations. First the parent-child interactions were observed while the family was having dinner. This was done for a period of three days. Second, the parent-child interaction was observed with three different problem-solving tasks. After all data were collected the research assistant rated the degree of inductive discipline strategies employed by the parent on a five-point scale. Ten Haaf and Janssens found moderate relations between inductive discipline assessed within the interview, observed inductive discipline (dinner and task situation), and overall ratings. They concluded that evidence exists for the validity of the measures.

Janssen (1990) also investigated the relation between reported behavior and actual behavior. In this research, he distinguished between four types of parental reactions. One of these types was giving information. The operationalization of

---

[11] We thank Prof. dr. C. van Lieshout and dr. M. Riksen-Walraven, Department of Developmental Psychology, University of Nijmegen who provided us with the videotapes.

giving information closely resembles our operationalization of inductive discipline. It includes a diversity of explanations and reasons. This type of behavior was assessed with an interview as well as by observing the parent-child interaction when the child tried to solve a puzzle (Wiggly Block). In the interview parents were asked how they would react on several hypothetical situations. Janssen found a significant relation between the information provided by the parent when observed with the child solving a puzzle and the disciplinary information provided by the parent in response to hypothetical situations (r (81) = .38, p < .05). Taken together, these studies suggest that there is a correspondence between parental self-reports about disciplinary behavior and their disciplinary behavior in real-life situations.

6   RESULTS

Analysis

The results of the study will be presented in seven sections. As already indicated at the end of chapter 4 the panel design (see Figure 4) allows us to study changes responding with the children's age. Therefore, the first section involves a description of the changes in moral internalization that occur across age and any sex differences in the children's responding. In addition, the interrelations among the different indicators of moral internalization will also be reviewed. In the second and third sections the variables of empathy and perspective taking will be considered (section 6.2), along with the parental discipline variables (section 6.3). Changes occurring with age and sex are examined. Linear relations between parental discipline and moral internalization will be the focus of the fourth section (section 6.4). The relative importance of inductive discipline strategies and victim-oriented disciplinary strategies to moral internalization will also be examined, involving separate analyses for mothers and fathers. Furthermore, evidence for a cause and effect relation between parental discipline and moral internalization is presented using Structural Equation Analysis (section 6.5). Given affirmation of Hoffman's thesis that parental discipline is an antecedent to moral internalization, the hypothesis that empathy and perspective taking mediate this relationship will then be examined in the sixth section. In section 6.6 the mediating role of the child's empathy and perspective taking in the relationship between parental discipline and the child's moral internalization will be tested. To assess the mediating role of empathy and perspective taking specification of a model is problematic. Three types of variables are relevant, i.e. parental discipline, the mediating variables of empathy and perspective taking, and the variables measuring moral internalization. These three types of variables are ordered representing a longitudinal sequence. Ideally, three measurement occasions are needed to test such a longitudinal sequence. Because only two measurements are carried out part of the model must be tested with cross-sectional data. Two patterns of relationships can be tested. First, the influence of parental discipline at time 1 on the child's empathic reactions and perspective taking at time 2 can be examined, which may in turn influence the child's moral internalization at time 2. Thus in this model the child variables are measured cross-sectional. Second, the influence of parental discipline at time 1 on the child's perspective taking at time 1, which influences future moral internalization (time 2) can also be examined. When evidence is found that discipline precedes moral internalization both patterns will be tested. Note that the last pattern is only tested with perspective taking as mediating variable because the assessment of empathy at time 1 proved to be invalid (see section 5.3.2). Finally, in the last section, some nonlinear relations between parental discipline and moral internalization are considered (section 6.7).

6.1   Descriptive statistics for the indicators of moral internalization

The perceived seriousness of the S.M.I.-stories

To further document the validity of the moral internalization indicators we first examined whether the stories in the S.M.I. were judged to be equally serious across the age groups. If we want to take reported guilt experiences across the cohorts as an indication of moral internalization the transgressions must be experienced as equally severe. We therefore asked the children to judge the severeness of the act in each story on a four-point rating scale (e.g., "How wrong is it to break another's toy?", "How wrong is it to deceive someone in a game?"; 0 = not wrong, 1 = little wrong, 2 = moderately wrong, 3 = very wrong).

Analyses of variance reveal young children judge the acts to be equally as wrong

Table 11   Mean judgment of the perceived seriousness of the act described in each S.M.I.-story for each cohort

act:	hurt someone					
	cohort 1	cohort 2	cohort 3	d.f.	F	p
T=1	...a	2.3	2.3	1, 98	0.04	n.s.*
T=2	2.3	2.1	2.4	2, 137	2.74	n.s.

act:	cheating					
	cohort 1	cohort 2	cohort 3	d.f.	F	p
T=1	...a	2.0	1.9	1, 98	0.25	n.s.
T=2	1.9	1.6	1.7	2, 137	1.42	n.s.

act:	breaking another's toy					
	cohort 1	cohort 2	cohort 3	d.f.	F	p
T=1	2.5	2.3	2.4	2, 141	0.93	n.s.
T=2	2.4	2.0	2.4	2, 137	6.99	.001

act:	taking away another's toy					
	cohort 1	cohort 2	cohort 3	d.f.	F	p
T=1	2.3	2.2	2.2	2, 141	0.15	n.s.
T=2	2.3	2.0	2.3	2, 137	1.93	n.s.

a   these stories were not included in the shortened version of the S.M.I.
*   p > .05

as older children (Table 11). An exception is the story in which a child breaks the toy of another child measured at time 2. Children in the first and third cohorts evaluated this act as more serious than children in the second cohort at time 2. The mean judgments of the other transgressions also show this trend. Nevertheless, these analyses show in general consistent nonsignificant results and therefore it is concluded that children at different ages do not significantly differ in their judgment of the severity of a particular act.

Developmental trends for the indicators of moral internalization

Because children internalize norms in the course of their development, we examined whether the older children receive higher scores for the indicators of moral internalization than the younger children. The guilt measure is a factor score (see section 5.4.1). A child's guilt score only reflects the child's rank relative to the scores of the other children (z-scores). We were also interested in the absolute scores for the children on the rating scales because these scores give us a better image of the answers given by the children. Therefore, we analyzed independently the original scores of the children on the three guilt measures: guilt intensity, concern for the victim, and use of justice principles. A Table showing the mean scores for each cohort on confession, resistance to pressure to deviate, and the three guilt measures at the two measurement occasions can be found in Appendix B (Table B-1). Before analyzing developmental trends the data provide the opportunity to get one more indication of the validity of the child variables. If moral internalization is measured validly then no differences should exist between the mean scores for two independent groups with a similar age. In this case it is hypothesized that the mean scores for cohort 2 at time 1 should equal the mean scores for cohort 1 at time 2. Likewise, the mean scores for cohort 3 at time 1 should equal the mean scores for cohort 2 at time 2. T-tests comparing mean scores of confession, resistance to deviation, guilt intensity, concern for the victim, and use of justice principles show no differences (p > .05).[1]

The mean scores for the variables confession and resistance to pressure to deviate for each cohort are high (for confession the lowest mean is 4.36 for cohort 3 at time 1; for resistance to pressures to deviate the lowest mean is 4.08 for cohort 1 at time 1; see Appendix B, Table B-1). That is, the means for these behavioral measures are skewed towards the higher end of the 1-6 scale. Developmental trends were analyzed cross-sectionally with a 3 (cohort) by 2 (sex) analysis of variance for each variable at each measurement point. The results of these analyses of variance can be found in Table 12. No significant cohort effects

---

[1]   For the comparison of the means of cohort 2 at time 1 with cohort 1 at time 2 and for the comparison of the means of cohort 3 at time 1 and cohort 2 at time 2 the t-values are respectively: confession t (93) = .52, t (99) = 1.61; resistance to deviation t (92) = .41, t (100) = .43; guilt intensity t (95) = .27, t (101) = .59; concern for the victim t (95) = 1.20, t (101) = .52; use of justice principles t (95) = 1.87, t (101) = .30.

Table 12 Three (cohort) by two (sex) analyses of variance with the indicators of moral internalization as dependent variables

dependent variable:	source of variation		d.f.	F	p
confession					
	T=1	cohort	2, 141	1.40	n.s.*
		sex	1, 141	12.74	.000
	T=2	cohort	2, 139	0.61	n.s.
		sex	1, 139	0.84	n.s.
resistance to deviate					
	T=1	cohort	2, 140	4.03	.020
		sex	1, 140	27.21	.000
	T=2	cohort	2, 138	1.75	n.s.
		sex	1, 138	10.11	.002
guilt intensity					
	T=1	cohort	2, 142	0.82	n.s.
		sex	1, 142	1.10	n.s.
	T=2	cohort	2, 144	3.95	.021
		sex	1, 144	2.43	n.s.
concern for victim					
	T=1	cohort	2, 142	4.57	.012
		sex	1, 142	3.85	n.s.
	T=2	cohort	2, 144	7.85	.001
		sex	1, 144	7.18	.008
use of justice principles					
	T=1	cohort	2, 143	26.50	.000
		sex	1, 143	5.52	.020
	T=2	cohort	2, 144	13.44	.000
		sex	1, 144	4.87	.029

Note All significant differences between cohorts have a significant linear component (p < .05). Use of justice principles at time 1 also has a significant nonlinear component (p < .05). For the remaining cohort effects no deviations from linearity are found.

Note No significant interaction effects between age and sex are found

* p > .05

for confession are found. Thus older children confess just as often as younger children after transgression. At time 1 it is found that girls scored significantly higher on confession than boys. However, this main effect is not present at time 2. Analyses of variance with resistance to deviation as a dependent variable show a main effect of cohort at time 1. However, the F-value is small and the cohort effect is not found at time 2. At time 1 as well as at time 2, moreover, analyses of variance show a significant sex effect. Girls scored higher on resistance to pressure to deviate than boys. When we consider the two behavioral measures, we can conclude that three analyses of variance show no cohort effect and the cohort effect for resistance to deviation found at time 1 is only small. If children internalize norms between the age of 5 and the age of 11, then main effects of cohort are expected. This is not found to be the case and it is suggested that when teachers use the other classmates as a frame of reference to rate a child any cohort effect may be neutralized. All but one of the analyses show that girls to score higher than boys on the two behavioral indicators.

To detect developmental trends in guilt we analyzed the scores on the three indicators of guilt. A small but significant cohort effect at time 2 is found for the intensity of the experienced guilt feelings (Table 12). Older children report more intense feelings of guilt than younger children. However, this main effect is not found at time 1. No sex effects are found. We also asked children the reasons for their feelings. The expressed concern for the victim and the number of justice principles employed by the children were rated. Most analyses show main effects of cohort and sex (Table 12). Young children are primarily concerned with themselves and older children are more often concerned for the victim and blame themselves of having violated their principles (see Appendix B, Table B-1). The small but significant main effects for sex indicate that girls show more concern for the victim (at time 2) and more often mention the importance of justice principles to explain their feelings than boys. This is in contrast to Thompson and Hoffman (1980) who reported no significant sex differences. Young children often mention egoistic reasons, such as fear for punishment or say that they feel guilty simply because they have broken a behavioral rule without referring to other reasons. Similar findings are reported by Thompson and Hoffman (1980) and Nunner-Winkler and Sodian (1988).

To summarize, almost no age effects are found for the behavioral indicators of confession and resistance to pressure to deviate. The lack of changes with age in the behavioral indicators could be explained by the possibility that teachers only rate the children on this scale relative to other classmates (e.g., taking the middle of the scale as the mean for the class). Older children also do not differ from younger children with respect to the intensity of guilt feelings they report after transgression, but the reasons for their guilt feelings do appear to change with age. Older children refer more often to the victim and stress the importance of justice principles in explaining their feelings. Finally, six of ten analyses show girls to score higher than boys on the indicators of moral internalization.[2]

---

[2]   Three (cohort) by two (sex) analyses of variance with the factor score for guilt as dependent variable reveal main effects of cohort (time 1, $F (2, 141) = 8.47$, $p < .001$; time 2, $F (2, 144) = 9.75$, $p < .001$) and sex (time 1, $F (1, 141) = 4.36$, $p < .05$; time 2, $F (1,144) = 5.85$, $p < .05$). Older children have higher scores on the guilt factor than younger children and girls score higher on guilt than boys. Cohort is linearly related to guilt. No significant nonlinear component is found.

Intercorrelations between the indicators of moral internalization

In the end we used three indicators of moral internalization (see chapter 5): the child's willingness to confess after transgression, the child's resistance to pressure to deviate, and the child's guilt experiences after transgression. Tables 13 and 14 show the correlations between these indicators at times 1 and 2. The Pearson correlations for the indicators with the age of the children affirm the cohort effects reported in the preceding section. Confession and age are not correlated and resistance to pressures to deviate is only positively associated with age at time 1 $(r (146) = .22, p < .05)$. Guilt and age are positively correlated at both meaurement occasions (time 1, $r (147) = .29, p < .05$; time 2, $r (150) = .32, p < .05$). Closer examination of the correlations reported in Table 13 and Table 14 reveals very high correlations between confession and resistance to pressure to deviate at time 1 as well as at time 2 (time 1, $r (146) = .68, p < .05$; time 2, $r (142) = .81$, $p < .05$). No or very low correlations are found between confession and guilt or resistance to pressure to deviate and guilt. When age is partialled out confession and resistance to pressure to deviate are not related with guilt. We conclude, therefore, that moral internalization is not a unitary construct. Other authors have

Table 13 Pearson correlations (upper triangle) and partial correlations controlling for the child's age (lower triangle) at time 1

	confession	resistance to deviate	guilt	age
confession	...	.68*	.07	-.03
resistance to deviate	.71*	...	.16*	.22*
guilt	.08	.11	...	.29*

* p > .05

Table 14 Pearson correlations (upper triangle) and partial correlations controlling for the child's age (lower triangle) at time 2

	confession	resistance to deviate	guilt	age
confession	...	.81*	.15*	.09
resistance to deviate	.81*	...	.12	.01
guilt	.13	.13	...	.32*

* p < .5

already suggested that moral judgments or feelings are not always expressed in behavior (e.g., Blasi, 1980; Eisenberg, 1982; Eisenberg, Shell, Pasternack, Lennon, Beller & Mathy, 1987; Radke-Yarrow, Zahn-Waxler & Chapman, 1983). Both confession and resistance to deviate are behavioral measures while guilt refers to reflections about feelings. The high correlations between confession and resistance to pressure to deviate, moreover, may have been inflated by the fact that the two indicators are subscales on the same questionnaire. Given this high correlation and the fact that both subscales constitute behavioral measures, the items on the two subscales are combined into a seven-item scale labeled 'moral behavior'. The internal consistencies Cronbach's alpha for this scale are found to be .87 at time 1 and .88 at time 2.[3]

6.2 Descriptive statistics for empathy and perspective taking

Developmental trends in empathy and perspective taking

Recall that only the measurement of empathy at time 2 proved to be valid. The mean scores for each cohort are presented in Table B-2 of Appendix B. According to Hoffman's model of empathy, in which empathy develops as a function of cognitive development and social experience age-related changes in empathy should be expected. A 3 (cohort) by 2 (sex) analysis of variance was performed to test for any significant developmental trends, the results of which can be found in Table 15. No significant differences between cohorts are found. The lack of age-related changes is confirmed by the nonsignificant Pearson correlation between empathy and the child's age (r (150) = -.11, p > .05). The analysis of variance reveals that girls and boys are equally emotionally responsive.

The mean scores for each cohort on perspective taking are also presented in Table B-2 of Appendix B. As for moral internalization no differences are expected between the mean scores of cohort 2 at time 1 and cohort 1 at time 2 and between cohort 3 at time 1 and cohort 2 at time 2. T-tests comparing mean scores for perspective taking show no significant differences between these subsamples (t-values are respectively: t (95) = .22, t (101) = .27, p > .05).

The 3 (cohort) by 2 (sex) analyses of variance for the data on each measurement occasion show the mean scores for perspective taking from the cohorts to differ (Table 15). This effect is affirmed by the significant correlations with age, moreover (time 1, r (149) = .64, p < .05; time 2, r (150) = .66, p < .05). Thus,

---

3 T-tests reveal no significant differences in the moral behavior of cohort 1 at time 2 and cohort 2 at time 1 (t (93) = -0.55, p > .05) and cohort 3 at time 1 and cohort 2 at time 2 (t (98) = 1.05, p > .05). Three (cohort) by two (sex) analyses of variance with moral behavior as dependent variable show main effects of sex (time 1, F (1, 140) = 22.25, p < .001; time 2, F (1, 138) = 3.95, p < .05). That is, girls are rated as showing more moral behavior than boys. No main effects of cohort are found (time 1, F (2, 140) = 1.65, p > .05; time 2, F (2, 138) = 0.71, p > .05).

Table 15 Three (cohort) by two (sex) analyses of variance with the indices of
moral internalization as dependent variables

dependent variable:		source of variation	d.f.	F	p
empathy					
	T=2	cohort	2, 144	0.69	n.s.*
		sex	1, 144	2.72	n.s.
perspective taking					
	T=1	cohort	2, 143	50.69	.000
		sex	1, 143	1.73	n.s.
	T=2	cohort	2, 144	63.00	.000
		sex	1, 144	2.26	n.s.

Note All significant differences between cohorts have a significant linear component (p < .05). No significant deviations from linearity are found.
Note No significant interaction effects between age and sex are found
*   p > .05

older children show higher levels of perspective taking than younger children. No
sex differences are found. Girls and boys do not differ in perspective taking.

We next compared the perspective-taking level of the children in our sample
with the levels of perspective taking found in Selman's theory. Selman (1976)
suggested that egocentric role taking (stage 0) is characteristic of 4 to 6-year-olds.
Six to 8-year-olds primarily show stage 1 reasoning. Children at about 8 to 10-
year of age are capable of self-reflective role taking (stage 2), whereas mutual role
taking (stage 3) is displayed only by 10 to 12-year-olds. To compare our results
with Selman's results, a global stage score, based on the child's average issue
score was computed. The child received a pure stage score (respectively 0, 1, 2 or
3) when the average issue score did not deviate more than 0.25 from the pure
stage score. Average issue scores that deviated more than 0.25 from the nearest
pure stage score were transformed into a global stage score somewhere between
the two pure scores (see Table 16). As can be seen in Table 16, most 5 to 6-year-
olds (cohort 1 at time 1) show stage 0 reasoning as well as stage 1 reasoning.
That is, these children sometimes show no differentiation of perspectives and
sometimes realize that people feel or think differently. Two years later, when the
children were 7 to 8-years-old most of them distinguished between different
perspectives (stage 1). However, they often failed to coordinate these perspectives. Nine to 10-year-olds (cohort 2 at time 2 and cohort 3 at time 1) appear to
reason transitionally between stages 1 and 2. Whereas 11 to 12-year-olds (cohort
3 at time 2) seem to be aware that people think or feel differently because each
person has his own perspective. They are also able to reflect on the self's behavior as seen from the parent's view. They seem to reason less authority-oriented

Table 16 Percentage of children reaching a given perspective-taking level of each cohort

global stage score	average issue score	cohort 1		cohort 2		cohort 3	
		time 1	time 2	time 1	time 2	time 1	time 2
0	< 0.25	9	2				
0-1	≥ 0.25 and < 0.75	59	11	16	2	2	
1	≥ 0.75 and < 1.25	30	74	62	44	36	11
1-2	≥ 1.25 and < 1.75	2	13	20	52	51	57
2	≥ 1.75 and < 2.25			2	2	9	30
2-3	≥ 2.25 and < 2.75					2	2
3	≥ 2.75						
Total		100%	100%	100%	100%	100%	100%

Note Cohort 1 at time 1 are 5 to 6-year-olds (n=47). Cohort 1 at time 2 (n=47) and cohort 2 at time 1 (n=50) are 7 to 8-year-olds. Cohort 2 at time 2 (n=50) and cohort 3 at time 1 (n=53) are 9 to 10-year-olds. Cohort 3 at time 2 (n=53) are 11 to 12-year-olds.

and become more aware that both parent and child can put the self in the other's place. None of the children in our sample, however, consistently showed stage 3 reasoning even though Selman predicted this level of reasoning to be displayed by 10 to 12-year-olds. Perhaps thinking about peers differs from thinking about parents (Damon, 1983). It may be more difficult to engage in perspective taking when there is a asymmetry in authority, as in the parent-child relation. Nevertheless, the general sequence of perspective-taking levels found in our data closely parallel those reported by Selman, which suggests that our assessment of perspective taking is valid.

The relation between empathy and perspective taking

Because of the lack of valid data on empathy at time 1, the relation between perspective taking and empathy could only be analyzed at time 2. No relation between perspective taking and empathy is found when using a Pearson correlation coefficient ($p > .05$). Empathy and perspective taking are found to be weakly but significantly related when the variance due to age is partialled out ($r (146) = .17$, $p < .05$). Empathy and perspective taking are theoretical constructs that mutually influence each other. On the one hand perspective taking can trigger an empathic reaction, on the other hand an empathic reaction can be modified by further information about the situation (e.g., placing oneself in the other's position; seeing that someone has been abused).

In the S.M.I. we asked the children to imagine that they were a bystander in the described situation and to report what they felt. Children's affective reaction was only coded as empathic when the children clearly condemned the act of the trans-

75

gressor or referred to the distress of the victim. Thus, the children had to realize that their feelings were in response to cues outside the self. The perspective-taking capacity necessary for such realization may be rather low. That is, the level of perspective taking needed for this cognitive act probably corresponds to stage 1 of Selman's stages. At stage 1, the child is aware that each person has a unique subjective personal perspective. Most children show at least this level of perspective taking at time 2 (see Table 16). That is, most children have the necessary cognitive capacity to show an empathic reaction in the S.M.I.-stories. Thus, when children do not show an empathic reaction this may not be a consequence of their perspective-taking ability. Differences in empathy scores, rather, may reflect differences in children's predisposition to react affectively. Another possible explanation for the variance in empathy observed here may be that some children are more willing to report their affective response than other children.

6.3   Descriptive statistics for inductive discipline and victim-oriented discipline

The perceived seriousness and recognizability of the D.T.I.-stories

In the interview assessing disciplinary styles, eight stories were used. We formulated stories thought to be relevant to the youngest children (5-year-olds) as well as to the oldest children (12-year-olds) in order to hold the behavioral situation as constant as possible. That is, the behavior of the child in each story must have the same significance for all parents. To control for this supposition all parents were asked to rate the seriousness of each situation if it were to happen to their own child. This seriousness was rated on a five-point scale ranging from not at all serious (0) to very serious (4). In addition, we asked whether a similar situation had ever occurred with their child. Table 17 shows the average seriousness for each situation as rated by the parents. Analyses of variance show three situations to be rated differently by the parents in each cohort. For example, at time 2 parents of children in cohort 1 tended to judge the situation in which their child cheats in a game as less serious than the parents of children in cohorts 2 and 3. Similar differences are found when the child snatches someone's toy (both at times 1 and 2) and when the child tears up another's favorite poster (only at time 2). As can be seen in Table 17 these differences are not necessarily due to the age of the children in the different cohorts. If this were to be the case, then we might expect some transgressions to be experienced as less serious with younger children, that is 7 to 8-years-old at time 2. However, when we consider the ratings for the 7 to 8-year-olds at time 1 (cohort 2) the transgressions are not judged as less serious when compared to the ratings for older children. Thus we cannot conclude that some transgressions are more or less serious depending on the age of the transgressor. Rather, we must conclude that some transgressions are rated as less serious by the parents in cohort 1.

Table 17 The perceived seriousness of each story used in the Disciplinary Technique Interview (means)

situation number[a]	short description of the act	time	coh. 1	coh. 2	coh. 3	F	p
				cohort[b]			
1	hurting someone	T=1	1.7	1.8	1.8	0.32	n.s.*
		T=2	1.5	1.8	1.6	2.58	n.s.
2	breaking someone's toy	T=1	1.4	1.5	1.4	0.58	n.s.
		T=2	1.4	1.6	1.5	1.08	n.s.
3	cheating in a game	T=1	1.3	1.6	1.4	2.07	n.s.
		T=2	1.2	1.5	1.6	4.27	.015
4	snatching someone's toy	T=1	1.4	1.8	1.9	5.44	.005
		T=2	1.3	1.8	1.8	8.08	.000
5	hurting someone	T=1	0.3	0.3	0.2	0.43	n.s.
		T=2	0.2	0.2	0.2	0.51	n.s.
6	tearing another's clothes	T=1	1.0	1.1	0.9	1.14	n.s.
		T=2	1.1	1.2	1.1	0.30	n.s.
7	making fun of a classmate	T=1	2.4	2.5	2.6	0.54	n.s.
		T=2	2.3	2.5	2.5	1.20	n.s.
8	tearing up someone's favorite poster	T=1	2.4	2.6	2.5	0.62	n.s.
		T=2	2.2	2.6	2.5	4.84	.009

a   The numbers correspond with the situations described in Table 8
b   Numbers of parents (mothers and fathers) in each cohort with complete data for
    perceived seriousness are 89, 95 and 98 for cohorts 1, 2 and 3 respectively at
    time 1 and 89, 95 and 96 for these cohorts at time 2.
*   p > .05

Table 18 Perceived seriousness of the stories in the Disciplinary Technique Interview when judged by parents (means)

time	cohort 1	cohort 2	cohort 3	boys	girls
			group[a]		
T=1	1.5	1.7	1.6	1.5	1.6
T=2	1.4	1.7	1.6	1.5	1.6

a   Numbers of parents (mothers and fathers) with complete data for the perceived
    seriousness in each cohort are 89, 95 and 98 for cohorts 1, 2 and 3 respective-
    ly at time 1 and 89, 95 and 96 for these cohorts at time 2.
    The number of parents with a son is 134 at both measurements. The number of
    parents with a daughter is 148 at time 1 and 149 at time 2.

Table 19 Main effects of the 3 (cohort) by 2 (sex) analyses of variance with the average perceived seriousness of the stories in the Disciplinary Technique Interview

time	main effect[a]	d.f.	F	p
T=1	cohort	2, 276	1.88	n.s.*
	sex	1, 276	2.01	n.s.
T=2	cohort	2, 274	6.44	.002
	sex	1, 274	0.08	n.s.*

a   No significant interaction effect of cohort by sex is found (p > .05)
*   p > .05

The average seriousness of the complete set of eight stories was also calculated. A comparison of the average ratings for the eight transgressions reveals a similar set of findings (Table 18). The overall judgments of parents in cohort 1 show the stories to be perceived as less serious when compared to the parents in the other two cohorts at both measurement times. Analyses of variance show only a cohort effect at time 2 (Table 19). When interpreted as an age effect, however, this effect is not confirmed by the data at time 1 (i.e., no significant cohort effect is found at this time).[4] Transgressions of boys and girls are judged as equally serious.

The percentage of children where at least one parent reported the situation to have occurred is shown in Table 20. As can be seen, some situations are more often recognized (e.g., situations 1, 3 and 5) than other situations (e.g., situation 4). Most situations, however, are recognized as applying to the child by most parents. The mean number of situations parents recognized is 6.3 at time 1 and 5.7 at time 2. The mean number of situations recognized for each cohort is shown in Table 21 (total of 8 possible). As can be seen, most situations applied to most children. The 3 (cohort) by 2 (sex) analyses of variance on the number of situations recognized as relevant by the parents show a cohort effect at both measurement times (see Table 22). That is, according to Table 21, situations

---

4   It can be hypothesized that the significant cohort effect at time 2 need not be interpreted as an age effect. The parents of cohort 1 seem to judge the transgressions as less serious than the parents of cohorts 2 and 3. If this is due to the age of the children (7 to 8-year-olds), then the parents of the 7 to 8-year-olds at time 1 (= cohort 2) should judge the transgressions equally as serious as the parents of the 7 to 8-year-olds at time 2. No evidence for this suggestion is found. A t-test comparing the means of cohort 2 at time 1 and of cohort 1 at time 2 provides evidence for the suggestion that the parents of cohort 1 experience the transgressions as less serious and that this difference is not explained by the age of the children (t (182) = 3.24, p < .01).

Table 20 The percent of children where at least one parent recognized the situation in the Disciplinary Technique Interview as applying to their own child

				cohort[b]	
situation number[a]	short description of the act	time	cohort 1	cohort 2	cohort 3
1	hurting someone	T=1	98 %	96 %	91 %
		T=2	92 %	88 %	91 %
2	breaking someone's toy	T=1	85 %	88 %	74 %
		T=2	85 %	82 %	66 %
3	cheating in a game	T=1	89 %	86 %	87 %
		T=2	96 %	90 %	83 %
4	snatching someone's toy	T=1	83 %	70 %	49 %
		T=2	57 %	52 %	38 %
5	hurting someone	T=1	96 %	100 %	96 %
		T=2	98 %	96 %	94 %
6	tearing another's clothes	T=1	66 %	80 %	64 %
		T=2	64 %	68 %	55 %
7	making fun of a classmate	T=1	72 %	78 %	70 %
		T=2	75 %	68 %	53 %
8	tearing up someone's favorite poster	T=1	68 %	54 %	55 %
		T=2	53 %	36 %	30 %

a   The numbers correspond to the situations described in Table 8
b   Numbers of children in each cohort are 47, 50 and 53 for cohorts 1, 2 and 3 respectively at both measurement times.

Table 21 Mean number of situations in the Disciplinary Technique Interview recognized by at least one parent as applying to their child

	group[a]				
Time	cohort 1	cohort 2	cohort 3	boys	girls
T=1	6.6	6.5	5.9	6.6	6.0
T=2	6.2	5.8	5.1	5.8	5.6

a   Number of children is 47, 50 and 53 for cohort 1, 2 and 3 for each measurement. The number of boys is 72 and girls is 78 for each measurement.

Table 22 Main effects of the 3 (cohort) by 2 (sex) analyses of variance on the number of situations in the Disciplinary Technique Interview recognized by parents as applying to their child

time	main effect[a]	d.f.	F	p
T=1	cohort	2, 276	3.7	.027
	sex	1, 276	4.9	.029
T=2	cohort	2, 274	5.2	.007
	sex	1, 274	0.7	n.s.

a   No significant interaction effect of cohort by sex is found (p > .05)

may be more frequently recognized by the parents of younger children than by the parents of older children. Moreover, the situations better apply to boys than to girls at time 1 (see Tables 21 and 22).

In summary, clear age-related changes in parent's ratings of the seriousness of transgressions are not found. Parents recognized most situations in the D.T.I. as applying to the child, although the set of situations appeared to be somewhat better suited to younger children. The perceived seriousness of the transgressions is not related to the child's sex. An analysis of the data of time 1 suggests that the set of situations might have been more relevant for boys than for girls (a finding not confirmed by the data from the second measurement occasion).

Age-related differences in inductive and victim-oriented discipline

As with the child variables, we first compared the mean scores from the parents of comparable groups to check the validity of our disciplinary measures. The mean scores for inductive discipline of cohort 2 at time 1 and cohort 1 at time 2 are equal, both for mothers and fathers (for mothers $t(95) = .07$, $p > .05$; for fathers $t(85) = .12$, $p > .05$; see Appendix B Table B-3 for complete data). Also no differences are found between the mean scores for inductive discipline of cohort 3 at time 1 and cohort 2 at time 2, for either mothers or fathers (for mothers $t(101) = .44$, $p > .05$; for fathers $t(87) = .24$, $p > .05$). This is also found to be true for victim-oriented discipline (for mothers $t(95) = .23$, $p > .05$ for the difference between the means of cohort 2 at time 1 and cohort 1 at time 2 and $t(101) = .96$, $p > .05$, for the difference between the means of cohort 3 at time 1 and cohort 2 at time 2. For fathers these t-values are respectively $t(85) = .53$, $t(87) = .38$, $p > .05$. See Appendix B Table B-4 for mean scores).

To assess any age trends in parental use of disciplinary techniques, 3 (cohort) by 2 (sex) analyses of variances were performed on each variable. With respect to paternal inductive discipline only a small but significant effect of sex at time 2 is found ($F(1, 144) = 4.01$, $p < .05$). Fathers tend to be more inductive towards girls than boys at time 2. At time 1 no differences between girls and boys are found with respect to paternal discipline (p > .05). Mothers of boys and mothers of girls do not differ in the amount of inductive discipline. No significant effects are found for cohort or sex on the victim-oriented scores of either fathers or mothers (p > .05).

The analyses indicate that the way in which parents discipline their children is not related to the age of the child. Parents may adapt their words to the child's cognitive level, but their overall preference for inductive messages and victim-oriented messages does not seem to change with the age of the child (5 to 12-years old). No significant differences between boys and girls are found, except for paternal inductive discipline at time 2.

The relation between maternal and paternal discipline

Use of inductive discipline strategies is found to be related to use of victim-oriented discipline strategies, both for mothers (time 1, r (149) = .39, p < .001; time 2, r (149) = .31, p < .001) and for fathers (time 1, r (131) = .45, p < .001; time 2, r (131) = .43, p < .001). Parents who frequently use inductive discipline also often use victim-oriented discipline. This is not surprising for these two discipline techniques are conceptually related. Explanations drawing the child's attention to the victim are inductive as well as victim-oriented. The operationalization of both disciplinary techniques also include overlapping categories. Pointing out the consequences of the transgression for the victim and stimulating the child to take the role of the victim are inductive as well as victim-oriented categories (see also operationalizations section 5.3.4).

We also analyzed the relations between maternal and paternal discipline. Pearson correlations show only a weak but significant relation between maternal inductive discipline and paternal inductive discipline at time 1 (r (131) = .23, p < .01). However, at time 2 no relation between maternal and paternal discipline is found (p > .05).

Where victim-oriented discipline is concerned, however, a weak positive relation is found at time 1 (r (131) = .22, p < .05) and at time 2 (r (130) = .15, p < .05). In other words, when the mother prefers to use victim-oriented messages the father also tends to rely on victim-oriented messages.

6.4 The relation between discipline and moral internalization

Linear relations between inductive discipline and the child's moral internalization

An important aim in this study is to explore the long-term influence of parent and child on each other. It is hypothesized that there is a relation between parental discipline and moral internalization. Before analyzing the long-term relations we examined whether parental discipline appears to be related to moral internalization within each measurement occasion. Recall that we also hypothesized the use of victim-oriented discipline strategies to stimulate the internaliza-

Table 23   Pearson correlations between parental use of inductive discipline and the child's moral internalization

| | | T=1 | | T=2 | |
		mother	father	mother	father
T=1	moral behavior	.00	-.04	.10	-.01
	guilt	.13	.10	.01	.09
T=2	moral behavior	-.04	-.10	.06	-.04
	guilt	-.01	.09	.09	.23*

* p < .05

tion of norms more than the diversity of techniques constituting the category of inductive discipline.

The intercorrelations between the cross-sectional assessments of inductive discipline and moral internalization are shown in Table 23. Significant correlations between maternal or paternal inductive discipline and moral behavior are not found, either at time 1 or at time 2 (p > .05), and only a significant correlation between paternal inductive discipline and guilt at time 1 is found (r (130) = .23, p < .05). These intercorrelations suggest that inductive discipline and moral internalization are not linearly related. However, the long-term effects of these variables may simply not be visible in the cross-sectional data. For example, parents who frequently use inductive discipline may stimulate the child's moral internalization but this effect may only be seen after an extended period of time. The correlations between data assessed at time 1 and the data assessed at time 2, thus, are also presented in Table 23. Again, however, no relations are found. That is, the use of inductive discipline at time 1 does not relate to the child's moral internalization at time 2. Likewise, the child's moral internalization at time 1 does not relate to the amount of inductive discipline used by the parent at time 2. This is found for mother-child dyads as well as for father-child dyads. This confirms the conclusion that inductive discipline and moral internalization are not related.

The correlations between inductive discipline and moral internalization may differ for the different subgroups, which means that a nonsignificant correlation can be expected when the subgroups are combined. For example, the influence of parents on their children may be particularly strong for young children and decline as the children grow older. If such substantial cohort effects exist an overall analysis (cohort membership ignored) will confound them. Consequently, independent analyses for each cohort and for each sex were conducted. Very few signi-

Table 24 Pearson correlations between parental use of victim-oriented discipline and the child's moral internalization

| | | T=1 | | T=2 | |
		mother	father	mother	father
T=1	moral behavior	.07	.07	.07	-.10
	guilt	.43*	.30*	.26*	.13
T=2	moral behavior	.06	-.04	.13	.12
	guilt	.06	.18*	.22*	.25*

* p < .05

ficant correlations are found (10% of the eighty calculated correlations had a probability of less than .05), and no cohort-dependent or sex-dependent patterns of correlation with some consistency could be detected (correlations for each subsample are included in Appendix B, Table B-5). In conclusion, the use of inductive discipline does not appear to be linearly related to moral internalization.

Linear relations between victim-oriented discipline and the child's moral internalization

Linear relations between the use of victim-oriented discipline and moral internalization were also analyzed using Pearson correlations. The results are presented in Table 24. As can be seen victim-oriented discipline does not appear to be related to the child's moral behavior at time 1 (p > .05). This is consistent with the findings in the preceding section which show parental inductive discipline and moral internalization to not be related. However, significant relations between victim-oriented discipline and guilt are found for both mothers (r (149) = .43, p < .05) and for fathers (r (131) = .30, p < .05) at time 1. When a parent frequently uses victim-oriented discipline techniques the child appears to show higher guilt scores. This holds for mothers and fathers as well. Moreover, the data of time 2 confirm these findings. Victim-oriented discipline and moral behavior are also not related, while a frequent use of victim-oriented discipline does appear to be associated with a high guilt level for both mothers (r (149) = .22, p < .05) and fathers (r (130) = .25, p < .05) at time 2. The consistency of these findings across time, moreover, suggest that the reported relations are valid.[5] Just as for inductive discipline, however, it is not unreasonable that

---

[5] The correlations within each cohort and within each sex are reported in the Appendix B (Table B-6). As for cross-sectional correlations, similar patterns are found. Some of the correlations are not significant (p > .05), but this may simply be due to the smaller sample size for that cohort.

victim-oriented discipline relates to future moral behavior and that our measures simply did not pick up on this fact. Table 24 shows no relation between moral behavior at time 1 and victim-oriented discipline at time 2, nor victim-oriented discipline at time 1 and moral behavior at time 2.

To summarize, we may conclude that victim-oriented discipline and guilt are related. Children who experience much guilt following transgression have parents who frequently use victim-oriented discipline. Similarly, children who do not feel very guilty following a transgression most likely have parents who do not direct the child's attention toward the distress of others. Moral internalization, operationalized as the amount of moral behavior, does not relate to the frequency of victim-oriented references, however. This suggests that mere victim-oriented discipline is not sufficient to create moral behavior; conversely, the child's moral behavior does not necessarily elicit a victim-oriented style of discipline. We consistently found no relation between the child's guilt experience and parental use of inductive discipline. The amount of explanations used by the parents to motivate children to change their behavior appears not to be related to children's moral behavior. These findings seem to confirm the suggestion that victim-oriented discipline is more important than inductive discipline.

6.5   Causes and consequences of parental discipline and moral internalization

The results from the correlational analysis of the cross-sectional data have already shown that the amount of victim-oriented discipline is related to the children's guilt experience and that the amount of victim-oriented discipline is not related to children's moral behavior. Up to this point, however, the causal direction of the relation between discipline and moral internalization has been ignored. In this section, therefore, we will examine these effects over time using structural equation modeling. Causal hypotheses will not be tested for inductive discipline and moral internalization for no relation between these two concepts was found. Similarly, causal hypotheses relating victim-oriented discipline and moral behavior will also not be tested. Only causal hypotheses for victim-oriented discipline and the child's experience of guilt will be tested in the following.

In these analyses, the cross-lagged correlations between guilt at time 1 and victim-oriented discipline at time 2 and victim-oriented discipline at time 1 and guilt at time 2 are examined. These cross-lagged correlations are presented in Table 24. For the father-child dyads there is a significant correlation between the use of victim-oriented discipline at time 1 and the child's guilt at time 2. The correlation between the child's guilt at time 1 and paternal use of victim-oriented discipline at time 2, however, is less strong and nonsignificant. As shown in Table 24 only the cross-lagged correlation between guilt at time 1 and maternal victim-oriented discipline at time 2 is found to be significant ($p < .05$), suggesting that the child's level of moral internalization may influence maternal disciplining rather than the other way around. Alternative explanations for this pattern of cross-lagged correlations are possible, however. For example, it is possible that guilt at time 1 concurrently affects maternal discipline and thereby leads to maternal discipline at time 2. A frequently used method for exploring the relative influence of parent and child is the method of cross-lagged correlations (e.g., Clarke-Stewart, 1973). This approach has also been frequently criticized (Cook & Campbell, 1979; Duncan, 1969; Rogosa, 1979). Rogosa (1979), for example, has suggested that the differences in the cross-lagged correlations may not only reflect different causal influences but also different variances. An alternative statistical technique that appears to be more appropriate for our needs and avoid the limitations inherent in cross-lagged panel analyses was therefore undertaken: Structural equation modeling.

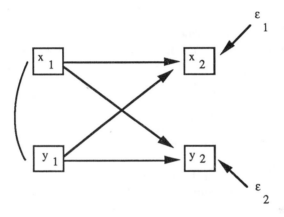

Figure 5   The starting model to test the causal direction

The model of causality specified in Figure 5 was taken as our original starting point (Plewis, 1985). In this model, x_1 and y_1 are measured variables at time 1 and x_2 and y_2 are measured variables at time 2. Variables x_2 and y_2 are assumed to be caused by variables x_1 and y_1, and variables x_2 and y_2 are assumed to have no causal link between them. It is recognized that x_1 and y_1 may not account for all of the variation in either x_2 and y_2 and therefore ε_1 and ε_2 are included as error terms. In the present model, variables are treated as if they were perfect indicators of the underlying concept. The inclusion of latent variables in the model results in a model that is seriously underidentified.

Several criteria may be used for judging the fit of the model. First the discrepancy between the hypothesized model and the observed data may be tested using a chi-square test. Since the chi-square statistic is a direct function of sample size, however, almost any model is found to not fit with larger sample sizes (Anderson, 1987). Hence, additional indicators will be used to judge the model. The second indicator will be a goodness-of-fit index. This index estimates the degree to which the model accounts for the variances and covariances characteristic of the data. The third indicator will be an adjusted goodness-of-fit index which adjusts the goodness-of-fit index to degrees of freedom and eliminates bias for models with few degrees of freedom. The fourth indicator is the root mean square residual, which is the average of the square of the residuals (mean of unexplained variances and covariances). The statistical distributions for the second to fourth indicators (goodness-of-fit index, adjusted goodness-of-fit index, and root mean square residual) are unknown; hence probability values cannot be assigned to the test statistics. Anderson and Gerbing (1984) assessed the effect of model characteristics on the distribution of these indicators, but only models for confirmatory factor analysis were tested and no direct values of the indices are formulated for our model without factor analysis. Notwithstanding these limitations, we deduced some guidelines for the interpretation of the indicators from the research of Anderson and Gerbing for our nonfactor analytic model. We chose the most conservative indicators for a model with two indicators for each factor and a sample size of 150 as a guideline for the interpretation of our indicators. We tentatively concluded that values above .94 for goodness-of-fit index, above .88 for adjusted goodness-of-fit index and below .064 for the root mean square residual are indicative of acceptable fits. A fifth criterion for judging the fit of our model is the statistical significance of each path coefficient (t-values) and the nonsignificance of the normalized residuals. Finally, the model is also evaluated by examining the amount of variance explained in the dependent variables.

We analyzed the data for the mother-child dyads and father-child dyads independently, and because guilt was found to be related to the child's age all correlations among the measures for victim-oriented discipline and guilt are controlled for age. The intercorrelations are reported in Table 25. This matrix served as the input to the LISREL-VI analysis (Jöreskog & Sörbom, 1981). In

Table 25 Intercorrelations among maternal victim-oriented discipline and guilt (controlled for age, n = 150)

		T=1		T=2	
		victim-oriented discipline	guilt	victim-oriented discipline	guilt
T=1	victim-oriented discipline	...	.46*	.39*	.08
	guilt		...	.25*	.30*
T=2	victim-oriented discipline			...	.22*
	guilt				...

* p < .05

86

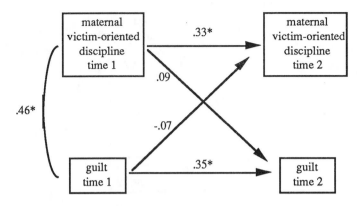

Note Goodness-of-fit indicators: $\chi^2(1) = 5.22$ (p = .022); goodness-of-fit = .982; adjusted goodness-of-fit = .824; root mean square residual = .052.
Proportion of variance in victim-oriented discipline time 2 explained = .16.
Proportion of variance in guilt time 2 explained = .09.

Figure 6   Structural representation of the relations between maternal victim-oriented discipline and guilt (n = 144)

Figure 6 the model generated by the LISREL-analysis is reported. As can be seen in Figure 6 the goodness-of-fit indicators do not consistently show an acceptable fit. The chi-square statistic shows that the model does not adequately fit the data (χ^2 (1) = 5.22, p = .022). The estimated value of the path from victim-oriented discipline at time 1 to guilt at time 2 and the path from guilt at time 1 to victim-oriented discipline at time 2 are called cross-lagged paths. An inspection of the path estimates shows that these cross-lagged paths do not reach significance (p > .05). Thus the way mothers discipline does not appear to influence the child's future guilt experiences. Also, no evidence is found for the hypothesis that mothers adapt their disciplining to the child's guilt experiences. The significant cross-lagged correlation between victim-oriented discipline at time 1 and guilt at time 2 (r (149) = .25, p < .05, controlled for age) therefore seems to be an artifact of an already existing association between discipline and guilt and the stability of these variables. This suggests a reduced model in which the variables are stable across time. In this model, victim-oriented discipline and the child's guilt at time 2 are completely explained by the relationship between these variables at time 1 and the stability of these variables. No cross-lagged paths are present in this model and this model seems to provide an adequate explanation of the data: χ^2 (3) = 6.96 (p = .073), goodness-of-fit index = .976, adjusted goodness-of-fit index = .921, root mean square residual = .060. However, modification indices suggest the existence of a relation between victim-oriented discipline and guilt at time 2, which cannot be explained by the correlation at time 1 and the

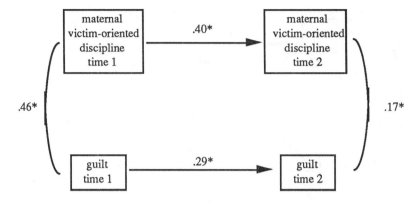

Note Goodness-of-fit indicators: $\chi^2(2) = 1.61$ (p = .448); goodness-of-fit = .994; adjusted goodness-of-fit = .972; root mean square residual = .027.
Proportion of variance in victim-oriented discipline time 2 explained = .16.
Proportion of variance in guilt time 2 explained = .08.

Figure 7   Structural representation of the reduced model of relations between maternal victim-oriented discipline and guilt (n = 144)

stability of victim-oriented discipline and guilt. As a consequence, the fit will once again be improved by taking into account the relation between the unexplained variances of victim-oriented discipline at time 2 and the child's guilt at time 2. This third model is shown in Figure 7 and provides a good fit for the data: χ^2 (2) = 1.61 (p = .448), goodness-of-fit index = .994, adjusted goodness-of-fit index = .972, root mean square residual = .027. The nonsignificant chi-square statistic and the fact that the values of the latter three indicators fall well within the acceptable ranges suggest that the measurement model is well-defined. The normalized residuals are nonsignificant; the stability-coefficients are significant. Although the variables show stability over time this need not imply that the parents and children have not changed over the two years. That is, only 16% of the variance in maternal victim-oriented discipline at time 2 and 8% of the variance in the child's guilt at time 2 is explained by the scores from two years prior.

Similar analyses for the existence of long-term relations between father's discipline and the child's guilt are done. Table 26 represents the intercorrelations between paternal victim-oriented discipline and the child's guilt with age partialled out. On both measurement occasions paternal victim-oriented discipline is found to be significantly related to the child's guilt. Both cross-lagged correlations are small and do not differ greatly. The correlation between the child's guilt score at time 1 and paternal victim-oriented discipline at time 2 is significant. A model with cross-lagged paths is tested first (Figure 5). The significant chi-square

Table 26 Intercorrelations among paternal victim-oriented discipline and guilt (controlled for age, n = 132)

| | | T=1 | | T=2 | |
		victim-oriented discipline	guilt	victim-oriented discipline	guilt
T=1	victim-oriented discipline	...	.26*	.51*	.13
	guilt		...	.15*	.30*
T=2	victim-oriented discipline			...	.27*
	guilt				...

* p < .05

statistic (χ^2 (1) = 7.58, p = .006) indicates that the data do not fit the model. The goodness-of-fit index is acceptable (.971), but the adjusted goodness-of-fit index is low (.714). The root mean square residual is acceptable (.063). Neither of the t-values of the cross-lagged paths are significant (p > .05) and, as with the mothers, the significant path coefficients between the scores of victim-oriented discipline at both measurement occasions and between the two guilt scores indicate the stability of these measures. In the second model, the full model (see Figure 5) is reduced by removing the cross-lagged paths. This model still provides a rather poor fit of the data (χ^2 (3) = 8.04, p = .045, goodness-of-fit index = .970,

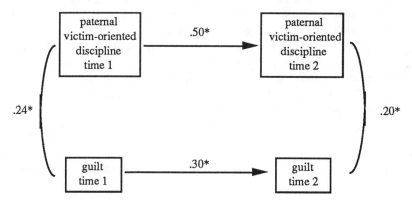

Note Goodness-of-fit indicators: $\chi^2(2)$ = 0.47 (p = .789); goodness-of-fit = .998; adjusted goodness-of-fit = .991; root mean square residual = .022.
Proportion of variance in victim-oriented discipline time 2 explained = .25.
Proportion of variance in guilt time 2 explained = .09.

Figure 8 Structural representation of the reduced model of relations between paternal victim-oriented discipline and guilt (n = 126)

adjusted goodness-of-fit index = .900, root mean square residual = .075).

This analysis suggests that a relation between the unexplained variance of victim-oriented discipline at time 2 and the unexplained variance of guilt at time 2 should be introduced and indeed this model (see Figure 8) provides a viable account of the observed data, which is shown by the nonsignificant chi-square statistic (χ^2 (2) = 0.47, p = .789) and the three goodness-of-fit indicators falling in the appropriate range. The stability-paths, moreover, are statistically significant (p < .05).

In summary, long-term effects of parents on children and children on parents are not found in this research. No evidence is found for Hoffman's hypothesis that parents influence the moral internalization of children.[6] On both measurement occasions victim-oriented discipline is found to be associated with the child's guilt experiences, and this is found to apply to mothers as well as fathers. This repeated finding suggests that the relation between victim-oriented discipline and guilt is valid. It should be noted that the path estimate between guilt on the first occasion and guilt measured two years later remains the same in the reduced model for mothers and the reduced model for fathers. This certainly does not indicate that the child's guilt experience does not change during two years. Only 8-9% of the variance in guilt measured at time 2 is explained by the earlier guilt level, however. Thus considerable changes within the total sample of children may have occurred. The guilt experience is also age related. Across the span of two years the children's guilt experiences may increase although the child's rank in comparison with the other children remains the same. The amount of victim-oriented discipline strategies a parent uses also shows stability. Fathers appear to be a little more consistent than mothers (regression coefficient mothers = .40; regression coefficient fathers = .50). It is concluded that although victim-oriented discipline and guilt are related, long-term influences across a period of two years are not observed. It is possible, however, that children and parents are continuously adjusting to each other and these reciprocal processes result in rather strong stability-coefficients over time, but not in significant cross-lagged paths. As suggested in chapter 2, such a dynamic model does not exclude the possibility of long-term influences. Such long-term influences, however, that are presumed to operate over a discrete time interval of two years are not found in this research.

---

[6]   It is possible that the relative strength of the long-term effects vary with the child's age. When the child is quite young the influence of parental discipline techniques on the child's moral internalization may be stronger than the influence of the child's moral internalization on discipline technique. Older children may nevertheless have an increasingly stronger influence on the parental discipline strategy. Examination of the correlations between the variables within each cohort and sex group revealed no such trends, however.

6.6 The role of empathy and perspective taking in the relation between victim-oriented discipline and moral internalization

One of the aims in this study was to find evidence for the mediating role of empathy and perspective taking in the relation between victim-oriented discipline and moral internalization. It is hypothesized that if victim-oriented discipline strategies influence moral internalization this is because pointing out the victim's distress stimulates the child to take the other's perspective and have empathy and thereby the child's level of moral internalization. The correlations of empathy and perspective taking to moral behavior and guilt are presented in Table 27, along with the correlations when age is partialled out. As before, we will first consider the relations within each measurement occasion.

Table 27 The relations between perspective taking, empathy, moral behavior and guilt (pearson correlation/partial correlation controlled for age)

		T=1 perspective taking	T=2 perspective taking	empathy
T=1	moral behavior	.25*/.25*	.12 /.08	.07 /.08
	guilt	.46*/.37*	.37*/.25*	.11 /.15*
T=2	moral behavior	.08 /.04	.14*/.13	.05 /.06
	guilt	.32*/.16*	.36*/.22*	.30*/.36*

* $p < .05$

As can be seen in Table 27, cross-sectional relations between perspective taking and both indicators of moral internalization (moral behavior and guilt) are found at time 1. Children showing a high capacity to take the perspective of another also show more moral behavior and experience more guilt than children with a low perspective-taking capacity. This relation is also found at time 2, although the Pearson correlation between perspective taking and moral behavior just reaches significance at time 2 and disappears when age is partialled out. Empathy could only be analyzed at time 2 and is found to be associated with guilt measured at time 2. No relation is found between empathy and moral behavior, however.

Thus, at a given point of time, perspective taking and empathy may be related to guilt and only perspective taking to moral behavior. This suggests that guilt and empathy are very closely related in part because feelings of empathy constitute a basis for guilt. When a child feels empathy for another and also realizes that he or she may have caused the damage, feelings of guilt may be the result (Hoffman, 1987). In turn, these feelings of guilt may motivate the child to behave morally. However, moral behavior need not be the result of feelings of empathy or feelings of guilt. For example, a child may know that the victim will not accept help (and therefore not act), or the child may want reinforcement (and therefore act). In these situations, that is, the child simply has to make the correct judgment.

Perspective taking and empathy are hypothesized to mediate the influence of parents on children's moral internalization, which predicts that relations between victim-oriented discipline and perspective taking and empathy must be found. As can be seen in Table 28, cross-sectional relations between victim-oriented discipline from both mothers and fathers and perspective taking exist. No relation between victim-oriented discipline and child empathy is found, however, which suggests that empathy may not mediate between victim-oriented discipline and moral internalization.

Table 28 The relations between perspective taking, empathy and victim-oriented discipline (pearson correlation)

		T=1 perspective taking	T=2 perspective taking	empathy
T=1	maternal victim-oriented discipline	.16*	.11	.02
	paternal victim-oriented discipline	.29*	.28*	.02
T=2	maternal victim-oriented discipline	.21*	.22*	.05
	paternal victim-oriented discipline	.03	.16*	.13

* $p < .05$

Long-term effects of victim-oriented discipline on the child's moral internalization are not found, which makes it difficult to test the hypothesis that empathy and perspective taking mediate between the two. An additional analysis was therefore attempted to tap the possibly mediating role of perspective taking in this relation. In section 6.5 victim-oriented discipline and guilt were shown to be related for both mothers and fathers at a given point in time but not longitudinally. We therefore decided to model the possibly mediating role of perspective taking in this relation using cross-sectional data. Of course, it would be preferable to use longitudinal data to estimate effects, but we now are concerned with making the best of things when no longitudinal effects over a two-year time lag are found.

Many studies try to make causal inferences based on cross-sectionally gathered data. As Gollob and Reichardt (1987) observed, these models fail to consider the influence of a variable on itself over time (stability). Furthermore,

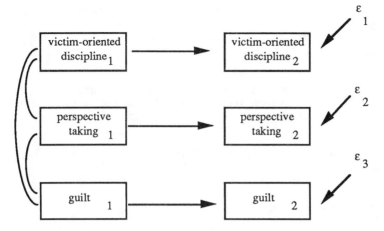

Figure 9   Model used to test the mediating role of perspective taking in the relation between victim-oriented discipline and guilt, with victim-oriented
discipline, perspective taking, and guilt at time 1 as causes of victim-
oriented discipline, perspective taking, and guilt at time 2

these models do not consider already existing associations between the variables
in the model. Already existing relations between such variables can be seen as
background variables. When these background variables are not part of the model,
the values of the paths will be overestimated. It is very difficult to estimate the
values of background variables (Gollob & Reichardt, 1987). For example, the
stability coefficient often depends on the time lag. Short lags produce high
stability coefficients, whereas long lags produce lower stability coefficients.
Because data from two measurement occasions are available in the present study,
however, we could start from the background relations present at time 1 and test
a model based on the data at time 2. Victim-oriented discipline and empathy
proved not to be related, which suggests that empathy also does not mediate
between victim-oriented discipline and moral internalization. Only perspective
taking, thus, may mediate between victim-oriented discipline and moral internalization. Such a model is tested and is presented in Figure 9. The variables are
treated as perfect indicators of the concept, and the model is tested separately for
mothers and fathers. The matrix presented in Table 29 is the input for the
LISREL-VI analysis of the mother-child dyads. Age was also controlled for. In
Figure 10 the model generated by the analysis of the mother-child dyads is
reported. The various goodness-of-fit indicators are also noted in Figure 10. As
can be seen, the model depicted in Figure 10 provides a good fit: χ^2 (7) = 10.10
(p = .183), goodness-of-fit index = .977, adjusted goodness-of-fit = .931, root
mean square residual = .055. The nonsignificant chi-square statistic, and the fact
that the values of the latter three indicators fall well within the acceptable ranges,

Table 29   Intercorrelations between maternal victim-oriented discipline, perspective taking, and guilt (controlled for age)

		T=1			T=2		
		maternal victim-oriented discipline	perspective taking	guilt	maternal victim-oriented discipline	perspective taking	guilt
T=1	maternal victim-oriented discipline	...	.23*	.46*	.39*	.18*	.08
	perspective taking		...	.37*	.22*	.34*	.16*
	guilt			...	.25*	.25*	.30*
T=2	maternal victim-oriented discipline				...	.24*	.22*
	perspective taking					...	.22*
	guilt						...

*   p < .05

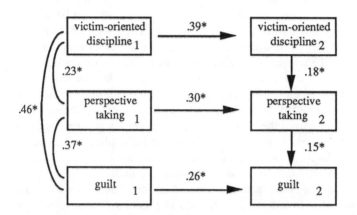

Note   Goodness-of-fit indicators: $\chi^2(7)= 10.10$ (p = .183); goodness-of-fit = .977; adjusted goodness-of-fit = .931; root mean square residual = .055. Proportion of variance in guilt time 2 explained = .10.

Figure 10   Structural representation of the model testing mediation of the relation between maternal victim-oriented discipline and guilt by perspective taking (n = 144)

Table 30 Intercorrelations between paternal victim-oriented discipline, perspective taking, and guilt (controlled for age)

| | | T=1 | | | T=2 | |
	paternal victim-oriented discipline	perspective taking	guilt	paternal victim-oriented discipline	perspective taking	guilt
T=1 paternal victim-oriented discipline	...	.22*	.26*	.51*	.21*	.13
perspective taking		...	.37*	.06	.34*	.16*
guilt			...	.15*	.25*	.30*
T=2 paternal victim-oriented discipline				...	.23*	.22*
perspective taking					...	.27*
guilt						...

* p < .05

suggest that the model is well-defined. Only 10 % of the variance in guilt at time 2 is explained by the other variables in the model. An inspection of the path estimates for the model shows low but significant regression coefficients for maternal victim-oriented discipline on perspective taking and perspective taking on guilt.

This indicates that a model in which victim-oriented discipline influences guilt by stimulating the child's perspective taking is confirmed.

This model is also tested for the influence of victim-oriented discipline by fathers on perspective taking and guilt. The data matrix for father-child dyads is presented in Table 30, and Figure 11 is the structural representation of this model. This model also provides a viable account of the observed data, as indicated by the nonsignificant chi-square statistic (χ^2 (7) = 9.32, p = .231) and the fact that the values of the three goodness-of-fit indicators all fall in the appropriate range. The model explains 10 % of the variance in the children's guilt scores at time 2. All of the regression coefficients, moreover, are found to be significant. It should be noted that the path estimates for victim-oriented discipline and perspective taking and perspective taking and guilt are almost equal to the regression coefficients found for the mother-child dyads.

It may be concluded that a model in which victim-oriented discipline stimulates perspective taking which in turn stimulates guilt fits the observed data. That is, a parent who frequently uses victim-oriented disciplinary techniques may stimulate perspective taking, and the better the child's perspective-taking capacity the more guilt the child may experience following a transgression. No evidence is found for the hypothesis that the child's capacity to react empathically medi-

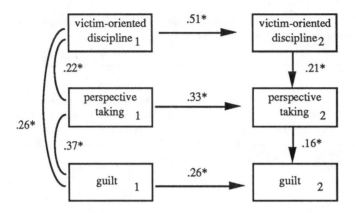

Note Goodness-of-fit indicators: $\chi^2(7) = 9.32$ (p = .231); goodness-of-fit = .976; adjusted goodness-of-fit = .929; root mean square residual = .051. Proportion of variance in guilt time 2 explained = .10.

Figure 11 Structural representation of the model testing mediation of the relation between paternal victim-oriented discipline and guilt by perspective taking (n = 126)

ates between victim-oriented discipline and guilt. It should be noted, however, that the regression coefficients found in the LISREL-analyses are very low but significant. Furthermore, a true causal structure should be tested on longitudinal data. Finally, the fact that this causal model is confirmed does not mean that other models cannot be confirmed; parental discipline might also be influenced by the child's guilt experiences.[7] Thus, no decisive answer can be given about the relative influence of parents and children on each other.

---

[7] One model is tested in which perspective taking at time 2 is assumed to influence guilt at time 2 and this guilt assumed to influence the amount of victim-oriented discipline used by the parent at time 2. Estimates of the values of background variables were based on the data at time 1. Low but significant regression coefficients are found for perspective taking on guilt (mother-child dyads the regression coefficient = .16; father-child dyads the regression coefficient = .16) and guilt on victim-oriented discipline (mother-child dyads the regression coefficient = .19; father-child dyads the regression coefficient = .21). The chi-square statistic is nonsignificant and the other goodness-of-fit indicators are acceptable, both for mother-child dyads and for father-child dyads. This indicates that the observed data also fit a model in which the child's level of moral internalization influences the parental disciplinary strategies.

6.7   Beyond correlations: Nonlinear relations between parental discipline and moral internalization

In the preceding analyses of relations between discipline and moral internalization we mainly have relied on correlational analyses to expose linear relationships. Pearson correlations may not be suitable for assessing relations between parental discipline and moral internalization, however. For example, independent and dependent variables may only be related for some children. Moral internalization is the process by which children become more and more motivated to consider the needs of others (cf. chapter 3). It is possible, however, that having automatized this activity, children are less likely to refrain from doing it. Thus, it may be suggested that children do not easily regress. Then, most children are hypothesized to show stability or progression in their moral internalization. We can check the plausibility of this statement by examining how many children display a regression in their moral internalization scores at time 2 when compared to their moral internalization scores at time 1. As we have seen in section 6.1, the absence of a developmental trend in moral behavior generally disconfirms the hypothesis that moral internalization is age-related. Two explanations can be offered for this result. Each child's behavior may have been rated only relative to peers in the same age range by the teacher; that is, the child was rated only relative to children of the same age rather than in general. It is also possible that moral internalization is only one of many factors that determine what shall be done. When the changes of guilt-scores across two years are considered, it is found that most children remained stable or progressed (the percentage of children who remained stable or progressed on the measures of guilt intensity, concern for victim, and use of justice principles are 58%, 64%, 74% respectively; that is, the absolute score on a guilt measure at time 2 minus the absolute score on that guilt measure at time 1 is zero or positive). Nevertheless, a considerable percentage of the children regressed. The guilt experiences may have been too globally assessed in this study.

If it should be true that children not easily regress and when it is assumed that moral internalization is influenced by the way parents discipline this may apply to parent-child dyads of which the parent starts using more inductive discipline techniques, respectively victim-oriented techniques. In addition, it may be suggested that when parents use less inductive or victim-oriented discipline techniques at time 2 this has no or little effect on the child's moral internalization. Thus, in analyzing these relations we are not interested in the subject's scores at time 1 but changes. Parents were divided into categories according to the degree of change in disciplining. Each parent was assigned to a category: Parents whose use of inductive discipline declined, was stable, or increased at time 2. A similar tripartition was made of parents for changes in victim-oriented discipline. The question was whether the children in these categories showed related changes. Similarly, it was asked whether the disciplinary styles of parents with children who showed more or less change in their level of moral internalization also changed. Therefore, children were categorized into three groups according to their changes in moral internalization. In this analyses the question was whether the parents in these categories showed related changes. With these nonlinear analyses we may find long-term relations that are not found with linear analyses.

Nonlinear relations between inductive discipline and moral internalization

Inductive discipline may be characterized in ways other than the proportion of inductive discipline used by the parent when attempting to change the child's behavior. Mothers in this study were divided into three categories based on the degree of change in their disciplinary styles. The position of each mother relative to the total sample of mothers is expressed as a z-score. This z-score is calculated for the assessment at time 1 as well as for the assessment at time 2. A comparison of these z-scores, thus, gives an impression of how the mother changed relative to the other mothers. A rather conservative measure was selected to indicate decrease and increase of disciplinary style, and a change in the z-score of at least 1 unit was required.

The first group consists of mothers who showed an increase in the proportion of inductive discipline (n = 27). The difference between their z-score at time 2 and their z-score at time 1 was 1 or more. The second group consists of mothers who remained relatively stable (n = 96). Their z-scores differed by less than 1 unit. Finally, the third group consists of mothers who declined in the proportion of inductive discipline they used (n = 27). The z-score for these mothers decreased by 1 or more units. There were no sex or cohort differences made in this classification. It was suggested that if parental inductive discipline relates to moral internalization, then the children of mothers who become more inductive should show a greater increase in moral internalization than children in other groups. Such analyses ignore the child's specific scores at times 1 and 2 and focus on the amount of change in moral internalization from time 1 to time 2. The change for each child is operationalized as the difference between the score at time 1 and the score at time 2. Changes in the indicators of moral internalization, moral behavior, and guilt are then compared.

Table 31 shows the mean change in the child's moral behavior with mothers who decreased their use of inductive discipline, remained stable in their use of inductive discipline, or increased their use of inductive discipline. For a correct interpretation of the mean changes of the indicators of moral internalization it should be noted that the children's scores of moral behavior can range between 1 and 6 and that the children's guilt scores are factor scores (see section 5.3.1). Analyses of variance indicate that mothers' changes in inductive discipline are not reflected in the child's moral internalization scores.

The fathers are divided into three similar groups (i.e., according to their z-score changes in inductive discipline). Twenty-three fathers decreased, 84 fathers remained the same, and 24 fathers showed a reduction in the use of inductive

Table 31 Mean changes in the child's moral internalization as a function of change mother's inductive discipline

	group I (decrease)	group II (stable)	group III (increase)	d.f.	F	p
moral behavior	-.12	.29	-.13	2, 137	2.95	n.s.*
guilt	-.18	-.05	.43	2, 144	2.39	n.s.

* p > .05

Table 32 Mean changes in the child's moral internalization as a function of change in father's inductive discipline

	group I (decrease)	group II (stable)	group III (increase)	d.f.	F	p
moral behavior	.32	.03	.38	2, 118	1.45	n.s.*
guilt	-.26	.01	.10	2, 126	0.66	n.s.

* p > .05

discipline.[8] Sex and cohort differences were not found for these groups. As can be seen in Table 32, the child's changes in moral behavior and guilt are the dependent variables. The results indicate that changes in the father's use of inductive discipline do not relate to changes in the child's moral internalization.

As already mentioned, the children are divided into three groups according to changes in the relative positions of their scores on moral internalization. This was done separately for moral behavior and for guilt. A chi-square analysis, calculated to test for any cohort differences, revealed that the children in cohort 1 showed less stability and more change in their guilt scores than the children in the other cohorts (χ^2 (4) = 17.35, p < .01). This relation was not found for moral behavior. No sex differences were found between the groups. For moral behavior, 20 children increased their relative position, 96 children were stable, and 24 children decreased. For guilt these numbers were 31, 89 and 27 respectively.[9]

---

[8] The sum of the subjects in each group sometimes is less than the maximum due to missing data. In this case, one father is missing.

[9] It should be noted where guilt is concerned that a stability in the z-scores over a period of two years does not imply that the guilt experience does not increase. Guilt is age-related. Thus the child's z-score is not only determined by the child's advanced or retarded moral internalization but also the age of the child. To eliminate this influence of age the z-scores of guilt and moral behavior were calculated within each cohort.

Table 33   Mean changes in parental inductive discipline as a function of change in child's level of moral behavior

	group I (decrease)	group II (stable)	group III (increase)	d.f.	F	p
mother	-.03	.01	-.01	2, 137	1.10	n.s.*
father	-.01	.00	-.01	2, 118	0.37	n.s.

* p > .05

Table 34   Mean changes in parental inductive discipline as a function of change in child's level of guilt experience

	group I (decrease)	group II (stable)	group III (increase)	d.f.	F	p
mother	-.03	.00	.02	2, 144	1.21	n.s.*
father	-.02	-.01	.03	2, 126	1.46	n.s.

* p > .05

The mean changes in the use of inductive discipline as a function of changes in the child's level of moral internalization are presented in Tables 33 and 34. The parent's scores represent the proportion of inductive reactions given in disciplinary encounters. Consequently, changes of the use of inductive discipline represent changes in proportions. Analyses of variance show maternal and paternal changes in inductive discipline not to reflect the children's changes in moral behavior and guilt. Thus, no relations are found between inductive discipline and moral internalization over a time interval of two years.

Nonlinear relations between victim-oriented discipline and moral internalization

The same procedure as with inductive discipline was followed in an examination of changes in victim-oriented discipline and moral internalization. Mothers were divided into three groups. The first group consists of mothers who increased the amount of victim-oriented discipline (n = 30). The second group consists of mothers who remained stable (n = 93). The third group consists of mothers who decreased the amount of victim-oriented discipline (n = 27). There were no sex or cohort differences in this classification. Table 35 shows the mean change in the level of moral internalization for each group. Mothers' changes in victim-oriented discipline are, to a limited extent, reflected in the changes associated with the children's moral internalization. For each variable, the highest mean change in moral internalization is found for children whose mothers had increased their use of victim-oriented discipline and the lowest mean score is

Table 35 Mean changes in the child's level of moral internalization as a function
of changes in mother's use of victim-oriented discipline

	group I (decrease)	group II (stable)	group III (increase)	d.f.	F	p
moral behavior	.03	.14	.25	2, 137	0.35	n.s.*
guilt	-.41	-.01	.56	2, 144	5.58	.005

* p > .05

Table 36 Mean changes in the child's level of moral internalization as a function
of changes in the father's use of victim-oriented discipline

	group I (decrease)	group II (stable)	group III (increase)	d.f.	F	p
moral behavior	-.19	.14	.50	2, 118	2.22	n.s.*
guilt	-.12	-.05	.17	2, 126	0.42	n.s.

* p > .05

obtained for children whose mothers had decreased their use of victim-oriented
discipline. However, the three parental groups differed significantly only on the
changes in guilt measure. T-tests show that the mean scores for group II and
group III differ significantly (t (144.0) = 2.38, p < .05), while the difference
between group I and group II is not significant (t (144.0) = 1.72, p > .05). This
suggests a nonlinear long-term relation between victim-oriented discipline and
guilt. That is, the guilt experience of children whose mothers increased the use of
victim-oriented discipline developed to a greater degree than the guilt experience
of other children. It appears, moreover, that a decrease in victim-oriented discipline does not necessarily imply a regression in experienced guilt. Note, however, that these conclusions are somewhat arbitrary; that is, the result is one just
significant t-value (p = .019) and one just nonsignificant t-value (p = .088).

When the data for the fathers are analyzed in a similar fashion, similar results are found (Table 36). Eighteen fathers showed a decrease in the use of victim-oriented discipline (group I). Ninety-one fathers remained stable (group II).
Twenty-two fathers increased their use of victim-oriented discipline (group III).
Cohort 3 is a little overrepresented in group I and a little underrepresented in
group III (χ^2 (4) = 9.93, p < .05). The mean changes of the moral internalization
scores show differences between the three groups. The highest mean change in
moral behavior and guilt is obtained for children whose fathers increased their use
of victim-oriented discipline over time, and the lowest mean scores are obtained

Table 37 Mean changes in parental victim-oriented discipline as a function of change in child's moral behavior

	group I (decrease)	group II (stable)	group III (increase)	d.f.	F	p
mother	.01	.01	.03	2, 137	0.22	n.s.*
father	-.02	.01	.03	2, 118	1.48	n.s.

* p > .05

Table 38 Mean changes in parental victim-oriented discipline as a function of change in child's level of guilt experience

	group I (decrease)	group II (stable)	group III (increase)	d.f.	F	p
mother	-.03	.02	.06	2, 144	5.45	.005
father	-.01	.01	.04	2, 126	2.47	n.s.

* p > .05

for children whose fathers used less victim-oriented discipline at time 2. In contrast to the analyses for maternal discipline, however, these differences do not prove to be statistically significant. In other words, no relations are found between changes in paternal victim-oriented discipline and changes in the child's moral internalization.

The mean change in the use of victim-oriented discipline by mothers and fathers as a function of children grouped according to changes in moral behavior and according to changes in guilt experience (for characteristics of these groups see preceding subsection) are presented in Tables 37 and 38. Although the differences were in the predicted direction, only the difference for changes in maternal victim-oriented discipline between groups divided according to changes in guilt are significant. The difference in mean changes between group I and group II is significant (t (144.0) = 2.48, p < .05). Thus mothers whose children's guilt scores regressed also slightly decreased their use of victim-oriented discipline (mean change in proportion victim-oriented discipline is -.03), while mothers whose children's guilt scores remained stable slightly increased their use of victim-oriented discipline (mean difference in proportion victim-oriented discipline is .02). The difference in mean changes between group II and group III is not significant. Thus, no differences are found between children who remained stable and children who, relative to other children, progressed.

In summary, no relation is found between changes in victim-oriented discipline by fathers and changes in the child's moral internalization. Also, no re-

102

lation is found between changes in victim-oriented discipline by mothers and changes in the child's moral behavior. Small but significant relations are found for changes in maternal victim-oriented discipline and changes in the child's guilt experiences. When mothers increased their use of victim-oriented discipline children's guilt experiences also increased relative to children of mothers who remained stable in their use of victim-oriented discipline. When mothers decreased their usage of victim-oriented discipline this is not reflected in the children's guilt scores when compared with children whose mothers did not change the amount of victim-oriented discipline used. Conversely, mothers of children who regressed in relative guilt also appeared to decrease their use of victim-oriented discipline when compared to children with a stable relative position. This indicates that relations between changes in the use of maternal victim-oriented discipline and changes in the child's development of guilt may exist over time.

The aim of the present research was to investigate the relationship between disciplinary techniques used by parents and the child's internalization of moral norms. This general aim was specified into three research questions. The first question concerned which disciplinary techniques (inductive discipline versus victim-oriented discipline) appear to be important in the relationship between parental discipline and moral internalization. The second question was whether the long-term influence of parental discipline and children's moral internalization is unidirectional. The third question was whether the child's capacity to react empathically or the child's perspective-taking ability mediate between parental discipline and the child's moral internalization (see chapter 4). In this chapter, the answer to each of these questions will be discussed.

7.1   The relation between discipline and moral internalization

The first question in this study concerned the relationship between parental discipline strategies and the child's internalization of norms. Before going into this matter some remarks will be made about the assessment of moral internalization. Four indicators of moral internalization were distinguished: confession, resistance to deviation, guilt, and internal judgment. When these variables are indicators of the same underlying construct, how are these variables related to each other? Children barely differed in the kind of judgments they made. A comparison of the answers given by the children in this study with research by Nucci (1981) and Davidson, Turiel and Black (1983), moreover, seemed to validate these results. We may conclude, therefore, that only children younger than about seven tend to give moral judgments motivated by authority figures or the (negative) consequences of a moral transgression for themselves. It is suggested, thus, that the degree of 'internal judgment' may be an accurate indicator of moral internalization for younger children. Internal judgment was excluded from further analyses.

The two behavioral measures of moral internalization (confession and resistance to deviation) were found to be highly correlated, but bore no significant correlation to measures of guilt. This suggests that moral internalization is not a unitary construct and that the latter three measures (confession, resistance to deviation, and guilt) reflect two, virtually independent, dimensions of morality: Moral behavior, which is the result of combining the two behavioral measurement scales, and guilt.

As the first dimension of moral behavior is concerned, it should be noted that behaviors associated with the moral behavior indicator are limited to the child's behavior in the classroom as reported by the teacher. Our measure of moral behavior (see chapter 5) may be of limited validity. That is, moral behavior may be domain-specific, and thus the child may act differently in the classroom than outside the classroom. In particular, the child may be motivated to behave morally in the classroom but not in other situations. Besides this suggested domain-specificity, we must take into account two other problems. First, teachers are asked to indicate the degree of resistance to deviate and the willingness to confess after transgression demonstrated by the child. The occurrence of such behaviors does not necessarily reflect the internalization of norms, however. The manifestation of this behavior may also represent compliance to external pressure or the seeking of social approval. Children do not deviate or confess after a transgression because they think that the teacher expects them to act in this way. This might also explain the lack of age-related changes in moral behavior. Second, the lack of age-related changes in moral behavior may also be the result of the teachers' frame of reference. That is, the children in each age range were rated only relative to other children in the same age range and not more generally.

In addition to moral behavior there is a second dimension of moral internalization: guilt. Guilt is a factor consisting of three measures: guilt intensity, concern for the victim, and the use of justice principles. Thompson and Hoffman (1980) regarded these measures to all be indicators of guilt experience. This is verified by the high correlations between the three guilt measures. Children with high scores on guilt report intense feelings of remorse, even when the transgression goes undetected, and do not worry about external punishments; they also emphasize the distress of the victim and the importance of mutual trust or personal rights. As a result, the factor guilt consists of an affective component (the experienced feelings of remorse after transgression) and a cognitive component (the rationale for those feelings). Nevertheless, the affective component was assessed by self report in the present study. We did not measure real affects. That is, guilt should not be seen as an affective measure here but a cognitive measure with an affective aspect.

Age-related changes are found for guilt. Older children experience more intense feelings of guilt, associated with concern for the victim and violation of basic justice principles. Younger children do not experience much guilt and are primarily concerned with the consequences of the transgression for themselves. They fear punishment when the parents might detect the transgression and are afraid that the victim might take revenge or not want to play with them anymore. This confirms the results reported by Thompson and Hoffman (1980), and similar findings are reported by Barden, Zelko, Duncan and Masters (1980) and by Nunner-Winkler and Sodian (1988). Nunner-Winkler and Sodian, for example, found most 4-year-olds in their study to predict happiness after committing an undetected transgression. Most of the 8-year-olds, however, predicted negative emotions and motivated this with morally-oriented reasons.

In our study, no relations are found between moral behavior and guilt. That moral judgments or feelings are not always expressed in behavior has often been observed (e.g. Blasi, 1980; Eisenberg, 1982; Eisenberg, Shell, Pasternack, Lennon, Beller & Mathy, 1987; Radke-Yarrow, Zahn-Waxler & Chapman, 1983). In reviewing studies of the relation between prosocial reasoning and behavior, Radke-Yarrow et al. (1983) observed that significant correlations in the .20 and .40 range can be found as well as no association whatsoever. According to Maccoby (1980) there are several reasons why moral cognitions and moral behavior may not go together. In concrete situations a number of implications of the act may be considered (e.g. other's needs, self-interest, information available about the situation, the presence of other persons). These considerations can cause a discrepancy between an intra-individual indicator such as guilt and an inter-individual indicator such as moral behavior.

The first question in this study concerned the relationship between parental discipline and the child's moral internalization. The hypothesis was that the use of victim-oriented discipline strategies relates stronger to the child's moral internalization than inductive discipline strategies. No relations are found between inductive discipline and the indicators of moral internalization, but victim-oriented discipline is found to be related to guilt. The strength of the relationships is not particularly strong, but the correlations replicated across the two measurements. These findings, moreover, appeared to be independent of the child's age and sex and held for mother-child dyads as well as father-child dyads. The findings verify Hoffman's suggestion that drawing the child's attention to the victim is most important for stimulating the internalization of norms (Hoffman, 1970). The conclusion that especially victim-oriented discipline strategies are related to guilt can be explained by the emphasis victim-oriented discipline strategies put on the victim's distress and by the demanding aspects which are often included in a victim-oriented disciplinary reaction.

Victim-oriented discipline is distinguished from inductive discipline because inductive discipline includes to a large extent only one-way communication strategies (i.e. didactic induction, according to Peterson and Skevington, 1988). Inductive discipline was operationalized as the proportion of reactions following transgressions in which the parent tried to motivate the child to behave differently by explaining (e.g. "If everyone did this the world would be a mess", "If you act like this you will lose all your friends"). Such explanations often do not challenge the child's existing point of view or stimulate the child to rectify his actions. Moreover, inductive discipline does not necessarily direct the child's attention to the other's distress and does not explain the nature of it. Victim-oriented discipline clearly directs the child's attention to the other's distress. Victim-oriented discipline was operationalized as stressing the consequences of the child's behavior for others, stimulating the child to take the perspective of another, and stimulating repair. By pointing out the needs of the other person, a parent may create a conflict between hedonistic needs and the needs of others, and such a

107

conflict may be of particular importance for stimulating moral internalization (Hoffman, 1975a).

A second characteristic of victim-oriented discipline that is not always present in the inductive message is the demand aspect. Hoffman (1970) assumed that without some communication of responsibility the child might respond empathically but dissociate himself from the causal act or deny it. Victim-oriented discipline not only informs the child about the victim's distress but also appeals to the child's responsibility by stimulating perspective taking and repair. Demandingness refers to behavior by which the parent makes an appeal to the child's responsibility, to mature behavior, to independence or to resolution of problems. A clear relation between demandingness and moral development has been documented, moreover (Maccoby, 1980). Victim-oriented discipline clearly communicates to the child that he is responsible for the distress of another person and that he must take the needs of the victim into account.

A third possible characteristic that differentiates between victim-oriented discipline and inductive discipline is the suggestion that the child repairs the damage or apologizes. With the use of victim-oriented discipline, the parent not only points out the situation of the victim to the child, but also communicates how the child might relieve the victim's distress. From this viewpoint, victim-oriented discipline may teach children that they can control their environment. Such perceived control may influence behavior beyond the parent-child interaction, moreover. For example, Skinner (1986) has suggested that the child's perceived control may take over or supplement the mother's role in guiding and regulating child behavior in problem-solving tasks. It can be speculated, therefore, that perceived control also plays a role in the child's moral internalization and moral behavior. In our study, however, no relation between victim-oriented discipline and moral behavior could be found. As already said before, the validity of the assessment of moral behavior can be questioned.

Although victim-oriented discipline is related to guilt, no relation between victim-oriented discipline and moral behavior could be found. Parents may influence the development of guilt by a guilt-inducing discipline technique such as victim-oriented discipline. However, they cannot guarantee the transformation of a guilt experience into moral behavior. A second possible explanation is that we measured compliance in addition to morally motivated behavior. There seems to be a relation between compliance and the parental use of power to force the child to behave differently (Saltzstein, 1976). When a parent uses many power assertive strategies (such as punishment or threatening the child) and does not give many explanations or reasons (and as a consequence the parent has a low score on victim-oriented discipline) the parent may cause the child to end the undesired behavior or to avoid this behavior. It also can stimulate the child to repair. However, the child is forced to act in that way by the parent. Therefore, the hypothesized relation between victim-oriented discipline and moral behavior need not to be found.

7.2 Causes and consequences of parental discipline and moral internalization

Across a period of two years no cross-lagged causal linear relations could be found between victim-oriented discipline and guilt. That is, maternal and paternal victim-oriented discipline on the first measurement occasion is found to be not related to guilt on the second measurement occasion two years later. A relation is found between initial guilt and maternal use of victim-oriented discipline on the second measurement occasion. Paternal use of victim-oriented discipline is found to be related with the child's guilt two years later. LISREL-analyses showed, however, that these relations could be explained by the cross-sectional correlation between victim-oriented discipline and guilt at time 1 and the stability of victim-oriented discipline and guilt over a time interval of two years. Cross-sectional relations between victim-oriented discipline and guilt are found at both measurement occasions for both mother-child and father-child dyads. When changes over time are related small relations are found between changes of maternal victim-oriented discipline and changes of guilt. Victim-oriented discipline and guilt appear to be related but there is little evidence for the existence of long-term influences. Only cross-sectional relations are found and a stability over time. Stability is indicated by the relation between the measures on separate occasions.

What mechanisms might account for the lack of a long-term relation between discipline and moral internalization? First, the age-range of the children in this study may not have been appropriate for examining the long-term relation between discipline and moral internalization. For example, the relation between discipline and moral internalization may already be established before the child's fifth year. Second, the lag between measurements may have been incorrect to capture long-term influences. Finally, little or no long-term relation between parental disciplining and the child's moral internalization may exist. A transactional model may better characterize the relation between these two variables.

The first explanation concerns the age of the children in this research. From the time a child starts interacting with the environment, parents try to influence the child's behavior. Parents try to comfort their child or ignore the child to make the child stop crying. Encounters with a moral norm also occur in early interactions with brothers, sisters and peers and as soon as the child understands verbal messages this content may influence the child. These interactions, moreover, all take place before five years of age. The relationship between the use of victim-oriented discipline and the child's moral internalization, thus, may be consolidated in the first five to six years. After this period, relations between victim-oriented discipline and guilt may be explained by the stability of the parental preference for victim-oriented discipline and the stability of the child's level of moral internalization (stability does not imply that the child's moral internalization does not change. As noted before stability of moral internalization refers to the stability of the position of the child on indicators of moral internalization relative to peers). In other words, the study of quite early parent-child interactions may be critical to the investigation of long-term relations between discipline and moral internalization.

As already noted, it is also possible that the lag between the two measurement occasions was either too long or too short to find cross-lagged relations. The literature contained no recommendations, and it is therefore possible that the time interval should have been extended to tap really long-term effects of parental discipline on moral internalization or vice versa. Conversely, the lack of cross-lagged relations might have been the result of a too long interval. In a period of two years, many things can happen that also reduce the correlation between the initial measurements and measurements two years later. Thus long-term influences may be found when another time lag is chosen. The use of repeated measurements across a somewhat smaller interval is therefore recommended for future research because both minor and major long-term changes can then be documented.

The third possible conclusion we offer is that long-term effects of parental disciplinary style on the child's moral internalization (or vice versa) simply do not exist. If we assume both the age of the children and the measured time interval to be correctly selected, then no evidence has been found for Hoffman's claim that parental discipline has a unidirectional influence on the child's moral internalization. Evidence for the converse, a unidirectional influence of moral internalization on parental discipline, was also not found; a bidirectional model of long-term influences was also not confirmed. These results raise questions about the utility of such a model and the cross-lagged design for understanding the relation between parental discipline and moral internalization.

In chapter 2 we mentioned two levels of possible influence: short-term effects and long-term effects. Long-term effects refer to the possible influence of the parent's preference for victim-oriented discipline on the child's internalization of norms over an extended period of time; they also refer to the possible influence of the child's level of moral internalization on the parent's preference for victim-oriented discipline over a period of time. That is, over a large number of interactions between parent and child. Short-term effects refer to the daily interaction between parent and child within a single disciplinary encounter. The course of a parent-child episode may be determined by both the parent's long-term preference for a victim-oriented style and numerous other variables: The value attached to change of the child's behavior by the parent, the parental perception of effectiveness of the reactions, the parental state of mind, the perception of the situation by the parent (e.g. the causal attributions), the child's immediate reaction following transgression, the child's capacity and willingness to listen to the parent, and the child's cognitive capacity, etc. It is plausible that a child who is startled by the distress of the other and demonstrates some guilt elicits a different reaction from the parent than the child who flees or simply denies the transgression. In such a way, the child may influence the parental reaction. Similarly, the parental reaction may also influence the child. For example, when a parent points out the distress of the victim and clearly explains the victim's situation to the child, this may stimulate the child to consider the perspective of the other. Maybe the child will try to repair. But if the child neglects this message the parent may choose another strategy to influence the child.

Within a single episode parent and child are interacting, searching for an optimal fit between the behavior of the parent and the child. It is therefore hypothesized that within a single episode both parent and child influence each other. Because of these enduring influences of each partner on the other the question of who influences whom within an episode may not be relevant anymore. It may become impossible to disentangle the reciprocal influences.

A particular interaction episode is not only determined by situational characteristics. The course of the interaction may be influenced by child characteristics such as level of moral internalization, cognitive development, and temperament, as well as by parental characteristics such as the parent's cognitions, expectations, and preferences for a particular discipline strategy. These characteristics are not easily changed. For example, results of a study by Roberts, Block, and Block (1984) indicated considerable continuity in the child-rearing orientations described by parents of children between the ages of 3 and 12. Individual episodes, therefore, may confirm already present cognitions, expectations, preferences, or behavioral tendencies rather than elicit change. Only minor changes in future preferences of a particular discipline technique and the child's moral internalization will take place. Consequently, every new episode can be considered as a continuation and confirmation of the preceding episodes. At best small changes in both preferences for victim-oriented discipline and moral internalization may occur as the result of a sequence of reciprocal interactions.

Finally, the child's level of moral internalization may not only be the product of episodes where the child transgresses and the parent tries to influence the child by using discipline strategies. In this study only such a reactive mode of disciplining is investigated. It is likely that there are much more episodes which have an effect on the child's moral internalization. For example, episodes where the parent (or another person) functions as a model for the child. Also episodes in which the parent reacts responsive to the child or initiates affective interactions with the child may play a role in the child's moral internalization. Similarly there may be much more episodes which have an effect of the parental use of victim-oriented discipline strategies. For example, the information the parent receives about the child or about childrearing may change the use of a particular discipline strategy.

We may conclude that no unidirectional long-term relation exists between use of victim-oriented discipline and moral internalization. Rather, these factors manifest themselves in every-day interactions and probably reciprocally influence each other. Child characteristics will affect not only the outcome of the socialization process, but also the parents' practices themselves, so that parents' and children's interrelationships are best viewed as 'transactional', with each partner continually influencing the behavior of the other. Several authors have suggested that a transactional model is perhaps the best model of child socialization (e.g.

Dodge, 1986; Gerris, 1989; Grusec & Lytton, 1988; Riksen Walraven, 1989; Sameroff & Seifer, 1983; Vuyk, 1986). Adoption of such a transactional model, however, suggests that the pursuit of unidirectional long-term relations between parental discipline and moral internalization by the child may be futile. Causes and consequences may be indistinguishable.

To summarize, no long-term effects from the child's moral internalization on the parent's preference for victim-oriented discipline are found. The cross-sectional relationship may be the result of a mutually regulating process. The actions and cognitions of each interaction partner are in part determined and modified by the actions of the other person. Such a transactional model was not formulated at the time this study was designed. As a consequence it is a post hoc explanation for not finding evidence for long-term causal effects in this study.

7.3 The role of empathy and perspective taking in the relation between victim-oriented discipline and moral internalization

In the LISREL-analyses only cross-sectional relations between parental victim-oriented discipline and the child's guilt are found combined with a stability of victim-oriented discipline and guilt over a two-year interval. Because no causal linear relations are found between victim-oriented discipline and guilt the mediating role of empathy and perspective taking could not be tested. Therefore we looked whether this model could be tested cross-sectionally. In correlational analyses, however, both empathy and perspective taking are found to be related to the child's experience of guilt. Children who show more empathy also experience more guilt. Children who show a higher level of perspective taking also experience more guilt. Perspective taking is also found to be related to the use of victim-oriented discipline. The children of parents who frequently use victim-oriented discipline have a higher level of perspective taking than the children of parents who do not frequently use victim-oriented discipline. Although it was predicted that the use of victim-oriented discipline would increase empathic behavior, empathy was not found to be related to the use of victim-oriented discipline.

These findings for empathy are puzzling. Empathy is found to be related to guilt, but empathy is not related to either age, perspective taking, or maternal and paternal victim-oriented discipline. Several explanations are possible for these findings. First, the lack of a relation between empathy on the one hand and age, perspective taking, and victim-oriented discipline on the other hand, may be due to a ceiling effect on the measure of children's tendency to react empathically. The situations used to assess children's empathy may have been too simple to adequately measure differences in empathy. Nevertheless, children's empathy scores positively related to their guilt scores. How can this be explained when this ceiling effect is valid? This may have been caused by the correspondence between the assessment of empathy and the experience of guilt. The concepts were assessed with the same instrument (S.M.I.), and it is possible that the child who reports empathic feelings is also likely to experience guilt. This may explain that, despite of the possible ceiling effect, the child's empathy and guilt scores are moderately related. This does not, however, explain why relations between guilt and perspective taking and between guilt and victim-oriented discipline are found and no relations for empathy. Perhaps, the stories in the S.M.I. are simply more adequate for assessing guilt than empathy.

A second possible explanation for the finding that empathy does not relate to the child's age may be that older children simply do not easily admit empathic distress in response to another's distress. As children get older they may be more embarrassed to show feelings of empathic distress. In addition to the lack of a correlation between empathy and children's age, this tendency might also explain why correlations between empathy and victim-oriented discipline, and perspective taking are not found. But this would not explain why the guilt scores are also not similarly suppressed, unless we assume that guilt has a rather strong cognitive component as well as an affective component. That is, the experience of guilt in this study may be less sensitive to social influences and therefore correlate more directly with age than empathy.

A third possible explanation is that victim-oriented discipline, perspective taking, and guilt are predominantly associated with cognitions whereas empathy is predominantly associated with affects. By using victim-oriented discipline, parents explain the perspective of the victim. This may directly stimulate children's perspective taking and this perspective-taking ability may, in turn, arouse guilt feelings and stimulate the children's cognitions about their guilt feelings. This third explanation results in a rather cognitive model of the relationship between the use of victim-oriented discipline and the child's moral internalization.

It is clear that none of the above-mentioned explanations can satisfactorily account for the findings concerning empathy in this study. Taken together, however, they may contribute to a better understanding of the findings.

A cross-sectional model is tested in which victim-oriented discipline influences perspective taking and perspective taking influences the child's guilt experiences. The cross-sectional data gathered at time 2 were then incorporated into the model already corrected for the relations existing at time 1. The data fit the model. Thus, the relations found at time 2 could not be completely explained by the relations found at time 1 and the stability of the variables. However, the regression coefficients for victim-oriented discipline on perspective taking and perspective taking on guilt are very low. The percentage of variance in the children's experience of guilt explained by these variables is also low. Nevertheless, the mediating role of perspective taking in the relation between discipline and guilt appears to be confirmed.

Note that the verification of a model in which victim-oriented discipline influences the child's guilt experience by stimulating perspective taking does not exclude the possibility that the child's moral internalization also influences the way parents discipline their children. That is, the data might also fit a model in which moral internalization mediates the influence of the child's perspective-taking capacity on the parental use of victim-oriented discipline. In any case, perspective taking appears to play a role in moral internalization.

7.4   Some concluding remarks

Hoffman (1975a) presented a persuasive theoretical argument for the dominant effect of parental discipline on children's moral internalization. In the present study inductive discipline strategies are distinguished from victim-oriented discipline strategies. It was hypothesized that the use of victim-oriented discipline in particular would be related to the child's moral internalization. A test of the cross-lagged model showed clear cross-sectional relations between the use of victim-oriented discipline and guilt. Evidence for a relation between parental discipline and behavioral indicators of moral internalization are not found, however. Inductive discipline appeared not to relate to moral internalization. In section 7.2, three possible explanations for this lack of long-term effects were considered. First, long-term effects of parents on children may only be detected with younger children or infants. Second, a different time interval may have been needed. Finally, the relation between discipline and moral internalization may be best characterized by a transactional causal model. However, as Vuyk (1986) has remarked, the existence of such a transactional relation between parental discipline and moral internalization will be difficult to verify.

How can a transactional model of parental discipline and the child's moral internalization therefore be empirically verified? We do not know possible solutions to this problem but we want to terminate this chapter with some speculations. First, consideration of the patterns of variability over time may be more fruitful than focusing on linear relations. The continuous nature of parent-child interactions and the hypothesized importance of cognitions, expectations, and attitudes suggests that the parent's victim-oriented discipline, the child's moral internalization, and the relation between these two variables may primarily show stability. Each new episode may be a confirmation of what has happened in the preceding episode. Changes in one partner over a number of episodes, moreover, may be directly associated with changes on the other partner. The transactions may result in an escalating feedback loop characterizing the parent-child. If over a period of time the parent uses less victim-oriented discipline and the child shows a lesser degree of moral internalization, a negative escalation can be said to have taken place. A positive escalation or spiral can be said to occur when a parent's disciplinary strategy becomes more victim-oriented and the child's moral internalization also becomes stronger relative to peers whose parents show a stable amount of victim-oriented discipline. It may be needed to investigate sequences of episodes in order to understand the transactional relation between discipline and moral internalization. This suggestion leads to the second and third suggestion offered below.

A second factor critical to the study of transactional relations will be the use of multiple measurements with shorter intervals. Lewis (1989) emphasized the need to study development with short ranges in order not to miss any possible discontinuities in development. He argued that rather than seeking prediction over wide intervals we should recognize that order may exist only within limits. When multiple measurements are used we can seek predictions across a wider interval without losing sight of the complex details.

A third factor to consider the transactional nature of the relation between parental discipline and moral internalization is the general pattern of social relations involving the parent and child (Linney & Seidman, 1989). It may be more fruitful to find variables that characterize the parent-child dyad in moral encounters. For example, general indicators of the moral climate in the family or the match between parental behavior and the child's moral internalization may be particularly useful. Theoretical assumptions in which reciprocity, or contingent social interaction, are considered to be essential aspect of stimulation that promotes the child's moral internalization may require variables that characterize the system. That is, it may be important to look for variables that characterize an episode on the level of the social system (e.g. dyad, triad) rather than just measuring individual variables.

Finally, if the lack of long-term influences can be explained by adopting an ongoing sequence of transactions, the existence of any correlation between victim-oriented discipline and moral internalization still has to be explained. Maccoby and Martin (1983) recommended, for example, research with infants to determine how a parent-child pair starts their relationship. Researchers may examine parental characteristics such as childrearing attitudes and child-centeredness before the child's birth and than consider how these characteristics interact with child characteristics in subsequent parent-child interactions. Research may also concentrate on how inborn child characteristics influence parent-child interactions. An example of such research is a study by Van den Boom (1988) showing that the infant's inborn irritability clearly influences the parent's reactions to the child. In Hoffman's theory about moral internalization the child's empathy plays a central role. Hoffman assumed that empathy is an inborn characteristic. Perhaps differences in the infants inborn capacity to react empathically also trigger different parental reactions and these parental reactions may constitute the basis for future disciplinary style and/or moral internalization.

115

REFERENCES

Anderson, J. (1987). Structural equation models in the social and behavioral sciences: model building. *Child Development, 58,* 49-64.

Anderson, J., & Gerbing, D. (1984). The effect of sampling error on convergence, improper solutions, and goodness-of-fit indices for maximum likelihood confirmatory factor analysis. *Psychometrika, 49,* 155-173.

Anderson, K., Lytton, H., & Romney, D. (1986). Mothers' interactions with normal and conduct-disordered boys: who affects whom? *Developmental Psychology, 22,* 604-609.

Aronfreed, J. (1976). Moral development from the standpoint of a general psychological theory. In T. Lickona (ed.), *Moral Development and behavior. Theory, research and social issues* (pp. 54-69). New York: Holt, Rinehart, & Winston.

Arsenio, W. (1987). *Affect and cognition in sociomoral development: an integrative model.* Paper presented at the biennial meeting of the Society for Research in Child Development, Baltimore.

Arsenio, W. (1988). Children's conceptions of the situational affective consequences of sociomoral events. *Child Development, 59,* 1611-1622.

Baumrind, D. (1980). New directions in socialization research. *American Psychologist, 35,* 639-652.

Barden, R., Zelko, F., Duncan, S., & Masters, J. (1980). Children's consensual knowledge about the experiential determinants of emotion. *Journal of Personality and Social Psychology, 39,* 968-976.

Bearison, D., & Cassel, T. (1975). Cognitive decentration and social codes: communicative effectiveness in young children from differing family contexts. *Developmental Psychology, 11,* 29-36.

Bell, R. (1968). A reinterpretation of the direction of effect in studies of socialization. *Psychological Review, 75,* 81-95.

Bell, R. (1971). Stimulus control of parent or caretaker behavior by offspring. *Developmental Psychology, 4,* 63-72.

Bell, R. (1977). Socialization findings reexamined. In R. Bell, & L. Harper (eds.), *Child effects on adults* (pp. 53-84). Hillsdale, N. J.: Erlbaum.

Belsky, J. (1984). The determinants of parenting: a process model. *Child Development, 55,* 83-96.

Belsky, J., Hertzog, C., & Rovine, M. (1986). Causal analyses of multiple determinants of parenting: empirical and methodological advances. In M. Lamb, A. Brown, & B. Rogoff (eds.), *Advances in the Developmental Psychology* (Vol. IV, pp. 153-202). New York: Erlbaum.

Blasi, A. (1980). Bridging moral cognition and moral action: a critical review of the literature. *Psychological Bulletin, 88,* 1-45.

Brook, J., Whiteman, M., Gordon, A., Brenden, C., & Jinishian, A. (1980). Relationship of maternal and adolescent perceptions of maternal child-rearing practices. *Perceptual and Motor Skills, 51,* 1043-1046.

117

Brunk, M., & Henggeler, S. (1984). Child influences on adults controls: an experimental investigation. *Developmental Psychology, 20,* 1074-1081.

Bryant, B. (1982). An index of empathy for children and adolescents. *Child Development, 53,* 413-425.

Buck, L., Walsh, W., & Rothman, G. (1981). Relationships between parental moral judgment and socialization. *Youth and Society, 13,* 91-116.

Bugental, D., Caporael, L., & Shennum, W. (1980). Experimentally produced child uncontrollability: effects on the potency of adult communication patterns. *Child Development, 51,* 520-528.

Chandler, M. (1973). Egocentrism and antisocial behavior: the assessment and training of social perspective-taking skills. *Developmental Psychology, 9,* 326-332.

Chandler, M., & Greenspan, S. (1972). Ersatz-egocentrism: A reply to H. Borke. *Developmental Psychology, 7,* 104-106.

Chapman, M. (1979). Listening to reason: children's attentiveness and parental discipline. *Merrill-Palmer Quarterly, 25,* 251-263.

Chapman, M. (1981). Isolating causal affects through experimental changes in parent-child interaction. *Journal of abnormal child psychology, 9,* 321-327.

Clarke-Stewart, K. (1973). Interactions between mothers and their young children: characteristics and consequences. *Monographs of the Society of Research in Child Development, 38* (6-7, Serial No.153).

Clarke-Stewart, K. (1988). Parents' effects on children's development: a decade of progress? *Journal of applied developmental psychology, 9,* 41-84.

Clarke-Stewart, K., & Hevey, C. (1981). Longitudinal relations in repeated observations of mother-child interaction from 1 to 2 1/2 years. *Developmental Psychology, 17,* 127-145.

Cook, T., & Campbell, D. (1979). *Quasi-experimentation. Design & analysis issues for field settings.* Boston: Houghton Mifflin Company.

Damon, W. (1983). *Social and Personality Development.* New york: Norton.

Davidson, P., Turiel, E., & Black, A. (1983). The effect of stimulus familiarity on the use of criteria and justifications in children's social reasoning. *British Journal of Developmental Psychology, 1,* 49-65.

De Veer, A., Janssens, J., & Gerris, J. (1988). 'Perspectief nemen', empathie en morele ontwikkeling. *Kind en Adolescent, 9,* 248-265.

De Veer, A., Janssens, J., & Gerris, J. (1987). *Het Socio-Moreel Interview.* Nijmegen: KUN, Empirische Pedagogiek.

Dodge, K. (1986). A social information processing model of social competence in children. In M. Perlemutter (ed.), *Minnesota symposium on child psychology* (Vol. 18, pp. 77-125). Hillsdale, N.J.: Erlbaum.

Duncan, O. (1969). Some linear models for two-wave, two-variable panel analysis. *Psychological Bulletin, 72,* 177-182.

Edelstein, W., Keller, M., & Wahlen, K. (1984). Structure and content in social cognition: conceptual and empirical analyses. *Child Development, 55,* 1514-1526.

Eisenberg-Berg, N. (1979). The development of children's prosocial moral judgment. *Developmental Psychology*, *15*, 128-137.

Eisenberg, N. (1982). *The development of prosocial behavior*. New York: Academic Press.

Eisenberg-Berg, N., & Hand, M. (1979). The relationship of pre-schoolers' reasoning about prosocial moral conflicts to prosocial behavior. *Child Development*, *50*, 356-364.

Eisenberg, N., & Miller, P. (1987). The relation of empathy to prosocial and related behaviors. *Psychological Bulletin*, *101*, 91-119.

Eisenberg, N., Shell, R., Pasternack, J., Lennon, R., Beller, R, & Mathy, R. (1987). Prosocial development in middle childhood: A longitudinal study. *Developmental Psychology*, *23*, 712-718.

Feshbach, N. (1979). Studies of empathic behavior in children. In B. Maher (ed.), *Progress in experimental personality research, vol. 8* (pp. 1-45). New York: Academic Press.

Fultz, J., Batson, C., Fortenbach, V., McCarthy, P., & Varney, L. (1986). Social evaluation and the empathy-altruism hypothesis. *Journal of Personality and Social Psychology*, *50*, 761-769.

Gerris, J. (1989). Gezinsonderzoek als multidisciplinair werkterrein. *Gezin*, *1*, 5-31.

Gerris, J., Vermulst, A., & Franken, W. (1988). Een interactionistisch georiënteerde interviewmethode. Een inventarisering van opvoedingssituaties die ouders als problematisch ervaren. In P. Schoorl, A. de Vries, & M. Wijnekus (eds.), *Gezinsonderzoek. Methoden van gezinsdiagnostiek* (pp. 75-110). Nijmegen: Dekker van de Vegt.

Gollob, H., & Reichardt, C. (1987). Taking account of time lags in causal models. *Child Development*, *58*, 80-92.

Goodnow, J. (1988). Parents' ideas, actions, and feelings: models and methods from developmental and social psychology. *Child Development*, *59*, 286-320.

Grusec, J. E., & Kuczynski, L. (1980). Direction of effect in socialization. A comparison of the parent's versus the child's behavior as determinants of disciplinary techniques. *Developmental Psychology*, *16*, 1-19.

Grusec, J., & Lytton, H. (1988). *Social development. History, theory, and research*. New York: Springer-Verlag.

Haan, N., Langer, J., & Kohlberg, L. (1976). Family patterns of moral reasoning. *Child Development*, *47*, 1204-1206.

Higgins, E. T. (1981). Role taking and social judgment: alternative developmental perspectives and processes. In J. H. Flavell, & L. Ross (eds.), *Social cognitive development: Frontiers and possible futures* (pp. 119-153). Cambridge: Cambridge University Press.

Hoffman, M. L. (1960). Power assertion by the parent and its impact on the child. *Child Development*, *31*, 129-143.

Hoffman, M. L. (1963). Child rearing practices and moral development: generalizations from empirical research. *Child Development*, *34*, 295-318.

Hoffman, M. L. (1970). Moral Development. In H. P. Mussen (ed.), *Carmichael's Handbook of Child Psychology, Vol. II* (pp. 261-369). New York: Wiley.

Hoffman, M. L. (1971a). Identification and conscience development. *Child Development, 42,* 1071-1082.

Hoffman, M. L. (1971b). Father absence and conscience development. *Developmental Psychology, 4,* 400-406.

Hoffman, M. L. (1975a). Moral internalization, parental power, and the nature of parent-child interaction. *Developmental Psychology, 11,* 228-239.

Hoffman, M. L. (1975b). Developmental synthesis of affect and cognition and its implications for altruistic motivation. *Developmental Psychology, 11,* 607-622.

Hoffman, M. L. (1975c). Altruistic behavior and the parent-child relationship. *Journal of personality and social psychology, 31,* 937-943.

Hoffman, M. L. (1976). Empathy, role taking, guilt, and development of altruistic motives. In T. Lickona (ed.), *Moral development and moral behavior. Theory, research and social issues* (pp. 124-143). New York: Holt, Rinehart, & Winston.

Hoffman, M. L. (1979). Development of moral thought, feeling, and behavior. *American Psychologist, 34,* 958-966.

Hoffman, M. L. (1982a). Development of prosocial motivation: empathy and guilt. In N. Eisenberg (ed.), *The development of prosocial behavior* (pp. 281-313). New York: Academic Press.

Hoffman, M. L. (1982b). Measurement of empathy. In C. Izard (Ed.), *Measurement of emotions in infants and children* (pp. 279-296). New York: Cambridge University Press.

Hoffman, M. L. (1983). Affective and cognitive processes in moral internalization. In E.T. Higgins, D.N. Ruble, & W.W. Hartup (eds.), *Social cognition and social development. A socio-cultural perspective* (pp. 236-274). New York: Cambridge University Press.

Hoffman, M. L. (1984a). Interaction of affect and cognition in empathy. In C. E. Izard, J. Kagan, & R. B. Zajonc (eds.), *Emotions, cognition and behavior* (pp. 103-131). Cambridge: Cambridge University Press.

Hoffman, M. L. (1984b). Parent discipline, moral internalization and development of prosocial motivation. In E. Staub, D. Bar-Tal, J. Karylowski, & J. Reykowski (eds.), *Development and maintenance of prosocial behavior* (pp. 117-137). New York: Plenum Press.

Hoffman, M. L. (1986). Affect, cognition, and motivation. In R. M. Sorrentino, & E. T. Higgins (eds.), *Handbook of motivation and cognition: Foundations of social behavior* (pp. 244-275). New York: Guilford.

Hoffman, M. L. (1987). The contribution of empathy to justice and moral judgment. In N. Eisenberg, & J. Strayer (eds.), *Empathy and its development* (pp. 47-80). Cambridge: Cambridge University Press.

Hoffman, M. L., & Saltzstein, H. D. (1967). Parent discipline and the child's moral development. *Journal of personality and social psychology, 5,* 45-57.

Howard, J., & Barnett, M. (1981). Arousal of empathy and subsequent generosity in young children. *Journal of Genetic Psychology, 138,* 307-308.

Iannotti, R. J. (1985). Naturalistic and structured assessments of prosocial behavior in preschool children: the influence of empathy and perspective taking. *Developmental Psychology, 21*, 46-54.

Janssen, A. (1990). "Ik zal je mores leren!". Een onderzoek naar de relatie tussen opvoedergedrag en de morele ontwikkeling van het kind. Unpublished doctoral dissertation, KUN, Nijmegen, The Netherlands.

Janssens, J., & Gerris, J. (1988). Sociaal milieu en reacties van ouders op disciplineringssituaties: een empirisch verklaringsmodel. *Pedagogische Studiën, 65*, 185-197.

Janssens, J., & Gerris, J. (in press). Childrearing, empathy and prosocial development. In J. Janssens, & J. Gerris (eds.), *Childrearing and the child's prosocial and moral development*. Lisse: Swets & Zeitlinger.

Janssens, J., Janssen, A., Bernaerts, M., & Gerris, J. (1985). *Disciplinering en situationele kenmerken*. Nijmegen: KUN, Empirische Pedagogiek.

Jay, S., & Farran, D. (1981). The relative efficacy of predicting IQ from mother-child interactions using ratings versus behavioral count measures. *Journal of Applied Developmental Psychology, 2*, 165-177.

Jöreskog, K. G., & Sörbom, D. (1981). *LISREL VI: Analysis of linear structural relationships by maximum likelihood, instrumental variables, and least squares method*. Mooresville: Scientific Software, inc.

Keller, B., & Bell, R. (1979). Child effects on adult's method of eliciting altruistic behavior. *Child Development, 50*, 1004-1009.

Kohlberg, L. (1976). Moral stages and moralization. The cognitive-developmental approach. In T. Lickona (ed.), *Moral Development and behavior. Theory, research and social issues* (pp. 253-265). New York: Holt, Rinehart, & Winston.

Kurdek, L. A. (1978). Perspective-taking as the cognitive basis of children's moral development: A review of the literature. *Merrill-Palmer Quarterly, 24*, 3-28.

Lepper, M. (1983). Social control processes, attributions of motivation, and the internalization of social values. In E. Higgins, D. Ruble, & W. Hartup (eds.), *Social cognition and development: A sociocultural perspective* (pp. 294-330). Cambridge: Cambridge University Press.

Lewis, C. (1981). The effects of parental firm control: a reinterpretation of findings. *Psychological Bulletin, 90*, 547-563.

Lewis, M. (1989). Commentary. *Human Development, 32*, 216-222.

Lickona, T. (1976). Research on Piaget's theory of formal development. In T. Lickona (ed.), *Moral Development and behavior. Theory, research and social issues* (pp. 219-240). New York: Holt, Rinehart, & Winston.

Linney, J., & Seidman, E. (1989). The future of schooling. *American Psychologist, 44*, 336-340.

Lowell Krogh, S. (1985). Encouraging positive justice reasoning and perspective taking. *The Journal of Moral Education, 14*, 102-110.

Lytton, H. (1979). Disciplinary encounters between young boys and their mothers and fathers: is there a contingency system? *Developmental Psychology, 15*, 256-268.

Maccoby, E. (1980). *Social development: Psychological growth and the parent-child relationship*. New York: Harcourt Brace Jonavovich.

Maccoby, E., & Martin, J. (1983). Socialization in the context of the family: parent-child interaction. In H. P. Mussen (ed.), *Carmichael's Handbook of Child Psychology : Vol. IV. Socialization, personality and social development* (pp. 1-101). New York: Wiley.

Nevius, J. (1984). Relationship of mothers' and ten-year-old sons' perceptions of maternal childrearing practices. *Perceptual and Motor Skills, 58,* 989-990.

Nucci, L. (1981). Conceptions of personal issues: a domain distinct from moral or societal concepts. *Child Development, 52,* 114-121.

Nunner-Winkler, G., & Sodian, B. (1988). Children's understanding of moral emotions. *Child Development, 59,* 1323-1338.

Peterson, C., & Skevington, S. (1988). The relation between young children's cognitive role-taking and mothers' preference for a conflict-inducing childrearing method. *Journal of Genetic Psychology, 149,* 163-174.

Piaget, J. (1965). *The moral judgement of the child*. London: Routledge and Kegan Paul.

Plewis, I. (1985). *Analysing change*. Chichester: Wiley.

Radke-Yarrow, M., & Sherman, T. (1985). Interaction of cognition and emotions in development. In R. Hinde, A. Perret-Clermont, & J. Stevemon-Hinde (eds.), *Social relationships and cognitive development* (pp. 173-190). Oxford: Clarendon Press.

Radke-Yarrow, M., Zahn-Waxler, C., & Chapman, M. (1983). Children's prosocial dispositions and behavior. In E. M. Hetherington (ed.), *Handbook of child psychology: Vol IV. Socialization, personality, and social development* (pp. 469-546). New York: Wiley.

Riksen-Walraven, J. (1989). Meten in perspectief. Een levensloopmodel als achtergrond bij het meten en beïnvloeden van gedrag en interacties. *Tijdschrift voor Orthopedagogiek, 28,* 16-33.

Roberts, G., Block, J., & Block, J. (1984). Continuity and change in parent's child-rearing practices. *Child Development, 55,* 586-597.

Roe, K. (1980). Toward a contingency hypothesis of empathy development. *Journal of personality and social psychology, 39,* 991-994.

Rogosa, D. (1979). Causal models in longitudinal research: rationale, formulation, and interpretation. In J. Nesselroade, & P. Baltes (eds.), *Longitudinal research in the study of behavior and development* (pp. 263-302). New York: Academic Press.

Rollins, B. C., & Thomas, D. L. (1979). Parental support, power and control techniques in the socialization of children. In W. R. Burr, R. Hill, F. I. Nye, & I. L. Reiss (eds.), *Contemporary theories about the family: Vol. 1. Research based theories* (pp. 317-364). London: Free Press.

Russell, A., & Russell, G. (1989). Warmth in mother-child and father-child relationships in middle childhood. *British Journal of Developmental Psychology, 7,* 219-235.

Saltzstein, H. D. (1976). Social influence and moral development. A perspective on the role of parents and peers. In T. Lickona (ed.), *Moral development and behavior. Theory, research and social issues* (pp. 253-265). New York: Holt, Rinehart, & Winston.

Sameroff, A., & Seifer, R. (1983). Familial risk and child competence. *Child Development, 54*, 1254-1268.

Selman, R. (1976). Social-cognitive understanding. A guide to educational and clinical practice. In T. Lickona (ed.), *Moral development and behavior. Theory, research and social issues* (pp. 299-316). New York: Holt, Rinehart, & Winston.

Selman, R. (1979). *Assessing interpersonal understanding: an interview and scoring manual in five parts constructed by the Harvard-Judge Baker Social Reasoning Project.* Boston: Judge Baker Guidance Center.

Shaffer, D., & Brody, G. (1981). Parental and peer influences on moral development. In R. W. Henderson (ed.), *Parent-child interaction. Theory, research and prospects* (pp. 83-124). New York: Academic Press.

Shantz, C. (1975). The development of social cognition. In E. M. Hetherington (ed.), *Review of child development research: Vol. V* (pp. 257-324). Chicago: University of Chicago Press.

Shantz, C. (1983). Social cognition. In P. H. Mussen, & E. M. Hetherington (eds.), *Handbook of child psychology: Vol. IV. Social Development* (pp. 495-550). New York: Wiley.

Skinner, E. (1986). The origins of young children's perceived control: mother contingent and sensitive behavior. *International Journal of Behavioral Development, 9*, 359-382.

Staub, E. (1979). *Positive social behavior and morality: socialization and development (vol. 2).* New York: Academic Press.

Strongman, K. (1987). *The psychology of emotion.* New York: John Wiley & sons.

Ten Haaf, P., & Janssens, J. (in press). Aspecten van ouderlijk opvoedingsgedrag: een validiteitsstudie. In J. Gerris (ed.), *Ouderschap en ouderlijk functioneren.* Amsterdam / Lisse: Swets & Zeitlinger.

Thompson, R., & Hoffman, M. (1980). Empathy and the development of guilt in children. *Developmental Psychology, 16*, 155-156.

Toi, M., & Batson, C. (1982). More evidence that empathy is a source of altruistic motivation. *Journal of personality and social psychology, 43*, 281-292.

Turiel, E. (1978). The development of concepts of social structure: social convention. In J. Glick, & K. Clarke-Stewart (eds.), *The development of social understanding* (pp. 25-107). New York: Gardner Press.

Turiel, E. (1983). *The development of social knowledge.* Cambridge: Cambridge University Press.

Turiel, E., & Smetana, J. (1984). Social knowledge and action: the coordination of domains. In W. Kurtines, & J. Gewirtz (eds.), *Morality, moral behavior, and moral development* (pp. 261-282). New York: John Wiley & Sons.

Underwood, B., & Moore, B. (1982). Perspective taking and altruism. *Psychological Bulletin, 91*, 143-173.

Van den Boom, D. (1988). *Neonatal irritability and the development of attachment: observation and intervention.* Unpublished Doctoral Dissertation, Rijksuniversiteit, Leiden, The Netherlands.

Van Westerlaak, J. M., Kropman, J. A., & Collaris, J. W. (1975). *Beroepenklapper.* Nijmegen: Instituut voor Toegepaste Sociologie.

Vuyk, R. (1986). *Opgroeien onder moeilijke gezinsomstandigheden.* Amersfoort: Acco.

Walker, L. J. (1980). Cognitive and perspective-taking prerequisites for moral development. *Child Development, 51,* 131-139.

Weir, K., & Duveen, G. (1981). Further development and validation of the social behavior questionnaire for use by teachers. *Journal of Child Psychology and Psychiatry, 22,* 357-374.

Yarrow, M., Waxler, C., & Scott, P. (1971). Child effects on adult behavior. *Developmental Psychology, 5,* 300-311.

Youniss, J. (1980). *Parents and peers in social development.* Chicago: University of Chicago Press.

Zahn-Waxler, C. Radke-Yarrow, M., & King, R. (1979). Child rearing and children's prosocial initiations toward victims of distress. *Child Development, 50,* 319-330.

Summary

In this dissertation part of Martin Hoffman's theory of child moral internalization is tested. The study focused on three main topics. First was the relation of inductive versus victim-oriented discipline to the child's moral internalization. Second was the relative strength of the long-term relations between parental discipline and moral internalization. Third was the mediating roles of the child's empathy and perspective taking in the relationship between parental discipline and moral internalization.

According to Hoffman, an infant is motivated by only hedonistic needs. A child must learn to take another's needs into account. A child who has internalized the norm to consider the needs of others may experience a conflict between hedonistic needs and the needs of others. Hoffman argued that parents' disciplinary strategies under such circumstances may be critical to children's moral internalization. In particular, the parents can place great constraints on the child because of their powerful position. In chapter two it is also argued that child characteristics such as temperament also affect parental behavior. According to Hoffman, however, this does not invalidate the argument that the long-term influence of parental discipline on moral internalization will be greater than the long-term influence of the child's level of moral internalization on parental discipline.

In chapter three the details of why parental discipline is of particular importance for moral internalization are outlined. Hoffman stressed the importance of directing the child's attention to the person who is victimized by the child. He also argued that use of an inductive disciplinary style is particularly important for moral internalization because parents provide the child with reasons for distress and give explanations to motivate the child's change of behavior. On the basis of both theoretical and empirical research it is suggested that the use of a victim-oriented disciplinary strategy may be of particular importance for the child's moral internalization. Such techniques are considered to be important because they may trigger empathic arousal in the child and may stimulate perspective taking. It is also shown that the child's empathic responses and perspective-taking capacity may be mechanisms by which parental disciplinary strategies influence the child's moral internalization.

In chapter four, the design of the study is presented. A cross-lagged panel design was undertaken with two measurement occasions and a time interval of two years. The sample of children was divided into three age groups or cohorts (5/6-year-olds, 7/8-year-olds, 9/10-year-olds), which allowed us to examine changes in moral internalization and parental discipline across a period of two years (within each cohort) as well as a period of six years (5/6-year-olds, 7/8-year-olds, 9/10-year-olds, 11/12-year-olds).

Chapter five outlines the general methodology. Data were gathered from 150 families: 150 mothers, 132 fathers, 72 boys and 78 girls. Discipline strategies for the parents were assessed using an interview, where each parent was asked how he or she would react to eight hypothetical situations. In each situation the son or daughter harmed another child. Four different aspects of moral internalization were operationalized. Two behavioral aspects were the child's tendency to confess/accept responsibility for deviant behavior and the child's resistance to pressure to deviate. To measure these, a questionnaire about the child's moral behavior was completed by the teacher. The third aspect of moral internalization was the experience of guilt following transgression. The fourth aspect was the child's propensity to make moral judgments independent of external sanctions. The Socio-Moral Interview was developed to assess the child's level of guilt and moral judgment. The results indicated most of the children to make moral judgments independent of external sanctions. This aspect was, therefore, excluded from further analyses, and we were left with three indicators of moral internalization. Confession and resistance to pressure to deviate proved to be highly correlated and were therefore collapsed into a single measure of moral behavior. Finally, the children were interviewed to assess their capacity for perspective taking and propensity to react empathically.

In chapter six the findings of this study are reported. Cross-sectional analyses showed that the use of inductive disciplinary strategies and the child's moral internalization to not be related, for either mother-child dyads, or father-child dyads. Victim-oriented discipline was found to be related to the child's experience of guilt, but not to the child's moral behavior. This was found, moreover, for both mother-child and father-child dyads. Furthermore, this was found at both measurement times. In other words, pointing out to the child that another person is in need is of particular importance for the child's experience of guilt.

The hypothesized long-term influences were analyzed using LISREL-VI. Evidence for Hoffman's hypothesis about the existence of long-term influences, however, was not found. Parental discipline did not appear to influence the child's moral internalization two years later. Similarly, the child's level of moral internalization was not found to influence future parental discipline. Rather, parental victim-oriented discipline and the child's moral internalization appeared to be quite stable across a period of two-years. In addition to these linear analyses some non-linear analyses were also performed. Changes in inductive discipline over a two-year interval and changes in moral internalization were found to bear no relation whatsoever. A weak relation between changes in the amount of victim-oriented discipline and changes in the child's moral internalization was found, however.

Because no causal linear relations were found between victim-oriented discipline and moral internalization, the mediating roles of empathy and perspective taking could not be tested. We tested therefore such a model cross-sectionally. Empathy and victim-oriented discipline were not found to be related. That is, empathy does not appear to mediate between victim-oriented discipline and guilt. However, the data were found to fit a model in which victim-oriented discipline influenced the child's perspective taking and, in turn, the child's experience of guilt.

Finally, in chapter seven, these findings are interpreted. The difference between victim-oriented discipline and inductive discipline for moral internalization is emphasized. It is concluded that behavior is not a direct, unambiguous, manifestation of moral internalization, which might explain the lack of relation between parental discipline and moral behavior as well as the lack of relation between the child's guilt experiences and moral behavior. Several explanations for the absence of a long-term relation between discipline and moral internalization are considered, and it is hypothesized that a transactional model may be the best characterization of this relation.

SAMENVATTING

In dit proefschrift wordt een gedeelte van Martin Hoffman's theorie over de morele internalisatie van kinderen beschreven en empirisch onderzocht. Het onderzoek was gericht op de beantwoording van drie hoofdvragen. Ten eerste werd gekeken naar verschillen tussen inductief disciplineren en slachtoffer-georiënteerd disciplineren in relatie tot de morele internalisatie van het kind. Op de tweede plaats werd gekeken naar de lange-termijn invloed van de wijze van disciplineren door de ouders op de morele internalisatie van het kind. Deze invloed werd verge- leken met de lange-termijn invloed van de morele internalisatie van het kind op de wijze van disciplineren door de ouders. Ten derde werd de rol van empathie van het kind en het perspectief nemen van het kind in de relatie tussen disciplineren en morele internalisatie onderzocht.

Volgens Hoffman wordt het gedrag van pasgeboren kinderen geleid door hedonistische behoeften. Het rekening houden met behoeften van anderen is het resultaat van een leerproces. Men zou kunnen spreken van morele internalisatie als het kind een intern conflict ervaart tussen hedonistische behoeften en de behoeften van een ander. Hoffman veronderstelde dat deze morele internalisatie een gevolg is van opvoeding. Hij hield een theoretisch betoog dat het handelen van ouders meer invloed heeft op de morele internalisatie van het kind dan omge- keerd. Deze sterke invloed van ouders op kinderen is volgens Hoffman het gevolg van de grotere macht die ouders hebben. Hoffman's betoog wordt gepresenteerd in hoofdstuk twee. Men zou kunnen tegenwerpen dat het handelen van ouders ook beïnvloed wordt door het kind. Bijvoorbeeld, door het temperament van het kind. Hoffman beaamde dat kinderen het gedrag van hun ouders beïnvloeden. Echter, volgens Hoffman impliceert dit niet dat zijn veronderstelling, dat het discipline- ringsgedrag van de ouder op lange termijn invloed heeft op de morele internalisa- tie, ongeldig is.

In hoofdstuk drie wordt nagegaan waarom Hoffman veronderstelde dat vooral disciplinering een rol speelt in de morele internalisatie van het kind. Hoffman suggereerde dat inductief disciplineren gerelateerd is aan morele internalisatie. Door uitleg te geven zou het kind gemotiveerd worden zijn of haar toekomstig gedrag te veranderen. Hoffman benadrukte dat het belangrijk is dat het kind gewezen wordt op het leed van het slachtoffer. Hoofdstuk drie bevat een kort overzicht van theoretisch en empirisch onderzoek naar de relatie tussen de wijze van disciplineren en de morele internalisatie van het kind. Geconcludeerd wordt dat waarschijnlijk vooral slachtoffer-georiënteerde disciplinering verband heeft met morele internalisatie. Doordat opvoeders wijzen op het slachtoffer kan het kind empathisch reageren. Bovendien kan het kind gestimuleerd worden om het perspectief van het slachtoffer in te nemen. Daardoor zou het kind gemotiveerd kunnen worden om een volgende keer meer rekening te houden met een ander. Volgens deze rationale zouden empathie en perspectief nemen de relatie tussen disciplineren en morele internalisatie kunnen mediëren.

In hoofdstuk vier wordt het design van de studie gepresenteerd. Het gebruikte design is een cross-lagged panel design met twee meetmomenten en met een interval van twee jaar tussen de twee metingen. De kinderen werden verdeeld in drie leeftijdsgroepen of cohorten (bij de eerste meting 5/6 jarigen, 7/8 jarigen, 9/10 jarigen). Twee opeenvolgende cohorten hadden een leeftijdsverschil van gemiddeld twee jaar. Dit design gaf de mogelijkheid om te kijken hoe de morele internalisatie en het ouderlijk disciplineren veranderen over een periode van twee jaar. Door het gebruik van drie cohorten werd het ook mogelijk om de morele internalisatie en het disciplineren te bestuderen over een periode van zes jaar (5/6 jarigen, 7/8 jarigen, 9/10 jarigen, 11/12 jarigen).

De opzet van het onderzoek staat in hoofdstuk vijf. Gegevens werden verzameld bij 150 gezinnen: 150 moeders, 132 vaders, 72 jongens, 78 meisjes. Via een interview werd gemeten hoe ouders reageren op normovertredingen van hun kind. De ouder werd geconfronteerd met acht hypothetische situaties. In elke situatie doet de zoon of dochter iets waardoor een ander kind benadeeld wordt. De ouder werd gevraagd hoe hij of zij zou reageren in zo'n situatie.

Vier, door Hoffman onderscheidden, aspecten van morele internalisatie werden geoperationaliseerd. Twee daarvan betreffen moreel gedrag. Ten eerste is dit de geneigdheid van het kind om na een overtreding de verantwoordelijkheid voor het eigen gedrag op zich te nemen. Ten tweede is dit de weerstand die het kind biedt tegen de verleiding om iets te doen dat niet door de beugel kan. Het moreel gedrag van het kind werd gemeten met behulp van een vragenlijst die ingevuld werd door de leerkracht van het kind. De samenhang tussen deze twee aspecten van morele internalisatie was hoog. Daarom werden de twee aspecten gecombineerd tot één indicator van morele internalisatie die moreel gedrag werd genoemd. De derde indicator van morele internalisatie heeft betrekking op de schuld die het kind ervaart na een overtreding. De vierde indicator van morele internalisatie vormt het moreel oordeel van het kind. Daarbij werd gekeken of het moreel oordeel vrij was van overwegingen waarin straffen of autoriteitsfiguren een rol spelen. Voor het bepalen van de schuldervaringen en het morele oordeel werd een interview, het Socio-Moreel Interview, ontwikkeld. Dit interview is bij de kinderen afgenomen. Uit de resultaten bleek dat de meeste kinderen een moreel oordeel gaven, dat onafhankelijk is van straf of autoriteitsfiguren. Daarom is besloten om deze indicator niet in de analyses te betrekken. Dus uiteindelijk zijn er twee indicatoren van morele internalisatie: moreel gedrag en schuld. De geneigdheid van een kind om empathisch te reageren en de vaardigheid van perspectief nemen werden eveneens bepaald door een interview met het kind.

In hoofdstuk zes staan de resultaten van het onderzoek. De relatie tussen disciplineren en morele internalisatie is eerst onderzocht op cross-sectioneel niveau. Zowel bij de data van de eerste meting als de data van de tweede meting werden geen verbanden gevonden tussen inductief disciplineren en morele internalisatie. Daarentegen werd er consistent een positieve relatie gevonden tussen het gebruik van slachtoffer-georiënteerde disciplinering en de schuldbeleving van het kind. Het gebruik van slachtoffer-georiënteerde disciplinering bleek niet samen te hangen met het morele gedrag van het kind. Dit werd gevonden zowel voor vaders als ook voor moeders. Bovendien was het patroon van correlaties bij de eerste en de tweede meting vergelijkbaar. Dus alleen slachtoffer-georiënteerde disciplinering was gerelateerd aan de morele internalisatie van het kind.

De hypothese dat disciplinering de morele internalisatie van het kind op lange termijn bepaalt, werd getest met behulp van LISREL-VI. Er is geen bevestiging gevonden voor het bestaan van lange-termijn invloeden. Dit geldt zowel voor de invloed van ouders op kinderen, als voor de invloed van kinderen op ouders. Wel bleek er een stabiliteit aanwezig in de wijze van disciplineren over een periode van twee jaar. Ook bleek er een stabiliteit in de mate van morele internalisatie over een periode van twee jaar. Naast een analyse van lineaire verbanden zijn er ook enkele analyses gedaan waarin gezocht werd naar de aanwezigheid van non-lineaire verbanden tussen disciplineren en morele internalisatie over een periode van twee jaar. Er werd gekeken of veranderingen in het gedrag van ouders gepaard gaan met veranderingen in de morele internalisatie van het kind. Wederom werden er geen relaties gevonden met betrekking tot inductief disciplineren en morele internalisatie. Er was echter wel een verband tussen een verandering in het gebruik van slachtoffer-georiënteerde disciplinering en een verandering in de morele internalisatie van het kind.

Omdat er geen causale verbanden gevonden zijn tussen slachtoffer-georiënteerde disciplinering en morele internalisatie kon de hypothese dat deze relatie gemedieerd wordt door empathie en perspectief nemen alleen getoetst worden op cross-sectioneel niveau. Er is geen relatie gevonden tussen slachtoffer-georiënteerd disciplineren en empathie. Een LISREL-analyse toonde aan dat de data overeenstemden met een model waarbij slachtoffer-georiënteerde disciplinering de morele internalisatie van het kind beïnvloedt via het stimuleren van perspectief nemen.

Tenslotte worden de resultaten van het onderzoek in hoofdstuk zeven bediscussieerd. De gevonden verbanden tussen disciplineren en morele internalisatie hebben alleen betrekking op de indicator schuld. Met betrekking tot moreel gedrag wordt geconcludeerd dat gedrag wellicht geen directe eenduidige manifestatie is van morele internalisatie. De verschillen tussen slachtoffer-georiënteerd disciplineren en inductief disciplineren worden bediscussieerd in het kader van het belang van deze disciplineringstechnieken voor de morele internalisatie van het kind. Voor de afwezigheid van lange-termijn invloeden worden verschillende verklaringen gegeven. Hierbij wordt de relatie tussen de wijze van disciplineren en de morele internalisatie van het kind gezien in het licht van een transactioneel model.

APPENDIX A

A story of the Socio-Moral Interview (version for boys):

The child is playing with his new ball.

The ball rolls into the road and a car runs over the ball. The ball is broken.

The child sadly walks away.

The child then sees his friend playing with a ball and starts crying.

He then snatches the ball on purpose.

Now his friend doesn't have a ball and starts to cry.

Another boy comes along.

133

APPENDIX B

Table B-1 Means and standard deviations for different indicators of moral internalization

Index: confession		mean	st. dev.	n	girls mean	girls st.dev.	n	boys mean	boys st.dev.	n
Cohort 1	T=1	4.40	.95	46	4.80	.67	23	3.99	1.03	23
	T=2	4.52	.83	47	4.56	.89	24	4.48	.78	23
Cohort 2	T=1	4.62	1.00	48	4.73	1.08	24	4.51	.92	24
	T=2	4.63	.93	48	4.67	.91	25	4.59	.97	23
Cohort 3	T=1	4.36	.74	53	4.60	.58	28	4.10	.82	25
	T=2	4.71	.77	50	4.82	.84	26	4.60	.68	24

Index: resistance to deviate										
Cohort 1	T=1	4.08	1.14	46	4.64	.97	23	3.52	1.02	23
	T=2	4.41	.97	46	4.64	.93	24	4.17	.97	22
Cohort 2	T=1	4.50	1.16	48	4.80	1.06	24	4.21	1.21	24
	T=2	4.75	1.08	50	4.91	1.13	26	4.58	1.01	24
Cohort 3	T=1	4.67	.96	52	5.08	.68	28	4.19	1.02	24
	T=2	4.46	1.01	48	4.82	.95	26	4.03	.94	22

Index: guilt intensity										
Cohort 1	T=1	1.96	1.72	45	1.83	1.51	23	2.09	1.94	22
	T=2	2.15	1.57	47	2.08	1.65	24	2.23	1.50	23
Cohort 2	T=1	2.23	1.35	50	2.42	1.25	26	2.03	1.46	24
	T=2	2.29	1.29	50	2.54	1.23	26	2.02	1.31	24
Cohort 3	T=1	2.45	1.44	53	2.74	1.26	28	2.12	1.58	25
	T=2	2.88	1.30	53	3.17	.97	28	2.55	1.55	25

Index: concern for the victim										
Cohort 1	T=1	2.41	1.37	45	2.30	1.39	22	2.52	1.37	23
	T=2	2.80	1.31	47	2.84	1.41	24	2.75	1.23	23
Cohort 2	T=1	3.13	1.36	50	3.47	1.20	26	2.75	1.45	24
	T=2	3.34	1.14	50	3.65	.98	26	3.00	1.22	24
Cohort 3	T=1	3.20	1.38	53	3.58	1.15	28	2.79	1.52	25
	T=2	3.75	1.19	53	4.11	.75	28	3.35	1.45	25

Index: use of justice principles										
Cohort 1	T=1	1.19	.97	46	1.13	.94	23	1.24	1.01	23
	T=2	2.06	1.23	47	2.00	1.28	24	2.12	1.20	23
Cohort 2	T=1	2.53	1.24	50	2.84	1.20	26	2.18	1.21	24
	T=2	2.82	1.28	50	3.16	1.18	26	2.45	1.30	24
Cohort 3	T=1	2.90	1.41	53	3.26	1.26	28	2.50	1.49	25
	T=2	3.31	1.17	53	3.61	.99	28	2.98	1.29	25

Table B-2 Means and standard deviations for empathy and perspective taking

Index: empathy

		mean	st. dev.	n	girls mean	st.dev.	n	boys mean	st.dev.	n
Cohort 1	T=1	...a	...	...	...	...	...	...	...	...
	T=2	.66	.23	47	.48	.24	24	.62	.21	23
Cohort 2	T=1	...	...	...	...	...	...	...	...	...
	T=2	.63	.20	50	.65	.19	26	.60	.20	24
Cohort 3	T=1	...	...	...	...	...	...	...	...	...
	T=2	.60	.26	53	.64	.21	28	.57	.30	25

Index: perspective taking

		mean	st. dev.	n	girls mean	st.dev.	n	boys mean	st.dev.	n
Cohort 1	T=1	.58	.29	46	.60	.27	23	.56	.31	22
	T=2	.95	.26	47	.95	.22	24	.94	.30	23
Cohort 2	T=1	.96	.34	50	1.04	.37	26	.88	.30	24
	T=2	1.24	.26	50	1.25	.29	26	1.23	.22	24
Cohort 3	T=1	1.26	.35	53	1.27	.40	28	1.25	.29	25
	T=2	1.56	.30	53	1.64	.35	28	1.47	.22	25

a   Only empathy scores assessed during the second measurement are available.

Table B-3 Means and standard deviations for inductive discipline used by mothers and by fathers

Mother

		mean	st. dev.	n	girls mean	st.dev.	n	boys mean	st.dev.	n
Cohort 1	T=1	.22	.11	47	.24	.12	24	.19	.10	23
	T=2	.21	.09	47	.24	.09	24	.19	.08	23
Cohort 2	T=1	.21	.11	50	.21	.11	26	.21	.11	24
	T=2	.19	.11	50	.20	.10	26	.19	.12	24
Cohort 3	T=1	.19	.08	53	.17	.08	28	.20	.07	25
	T=2	.20	.10	53	.22	.09	.28	.18	.11	25

Father

		mean	st. dev.	n	girls mean	st.dev.	n	boys mean	st.dev.	n
Cohort 1	T=1	.17	.11	42	.18	.13	21	.16	.09	21
	T=2	.14	.10	42	.15	.10	21	.13	.11	21
Cohort 2	T=1	.14	.09	45	.15	.10	24	.13	.08	21
	T=2	.14	.09	44	.12	.09	24	.17	.10	20
Cohort 3	T=1	.15	.10	45	.14	.10	25	.15	.09	20
	T=2	.17	.12	45	.18	.13	25	.15	.11	20

Table B-4 Means and standard deviations for victim-oriented discipline used by mothers and by fathers

Mother		mean	st. dev.	n	girls mean	st.dev.	n	boys mean	st.dev.	n
Cohort 1	T=1	.21	.10	47	.24	.10	24	.19	.10	23
	T=2	.23	.10	47	.23	.10	24	.22	.09	23
Cohort 2	T=1	.22	.10	50	.20	.11	26	.24	.10	24
	T=2	.23	.10	50	.20	.09	26	.25	.10	24
Cohort 3	T=1	.21	.10	53	.21	.10	28	.21	.10	25
	T=2	.24	.09	53	.24	.09	.28	.24	.09	25

Father		mean	st. dev.	n	girls mean	st.dev.	n	boys mean	st.dev.	n
Cohort 1	T=1	.16	.09	42	.16	.10	21	.15	.09	21
	T=2	.19	.09	42	.18	.09	21	.20	.10	21
Cohort 2	T=1	.18	.08	45	.18	.07	24	.18	.08	21
	T=2	.21	.08	44	.19	.08	24	.23	.09	20
Cohort 3	T=1	.20	.10	45	.20	.11	25	.19	.10	20
	T=2	.18	.11	45	.18	.11	25	.17	.12	20

Table B-5 Pearson correlations for parental use of inductive discipline and the level of moral internalization for boys, girls, cohort 1, cohort 2 and cohort 3

| | | | T=1 | | T=2 | |
			mother	father	mother	father
boys	T=1	moral behavior	.14	-.08	.11	-.05
		guilt	.24*	.21	.05	.09
	T=2	moral behavior	-.04	-.19	.04	.02
		guilt	.02	.09	-.01	.17
girls	T=1	moral behavior	-.17	-.05	-.01	.01
		guilt	.02	-.02	-.09	.09
	T=2	moral behavior	-.06	-.05	.04	-.10
		guilt	-.06	.07	.15	.29*
cohort 1	T=1	moral behavior	.07	.02	.28*	.04
		guilt	.20	.19	-.06	.19
	T=2	moral behavior	-.14	.14	.10	-.03
		guilt	.22	.22	.08	.49*
cohort 2	T=1	moral behavior	.03	-.03	.01	-.03
		guilt	.31*	.16	.06	-.06
	T=2	moral behavior	.12	-.11	.20	.18
		guilt	.02	-.07	.29*	.05
cohort 3	T=1	moral behavior	-.15	-.05	.10	-.08
		guilt	-.01	.09	.06	.11
	T=2	moral behavior	-.15	-.31*	-.11	-.27*
		guilt	-.21	.21	-.03	.10

Note The number of subjects within each subsample are:
72 boys with 72 mothers and 62 fathers
78 girls with 78 mothers and 70 fathers
cohort 1: 47 children, 47 mothers, 42 fathers
cohort 2: 50 children, 50 mothers, 45 fathers
cohort 3: 53 children, 53 mothers, 45 fathers
* p < .05

Table B-6 Pearson correlations for parental use of victim-oriented discipline and level of moral internalization for boys, girls, cohort 1, cohort 2 and cohort 3

			T=1 mother	T=1 father	T=2 mother	T=2 father
boys	T=1	moral behavior	.18	.17	.12	.00
		guilt	.52*	.28*	.27*	.14
	T=2	moral behavior	.25*	-.06	.22	.16
		guilt	.32*	.13	.20*	.34*
girls	T=1	moral behavior	-.06	-.07	.09	.03
		guilt	.35*	.31*	.28*	.17
	T=2	moral behavior	-.09	-.03	.07	.10
		guilt	-.02	.15	.28*	.19
cohort 1	T=1	moral behavior	.14	.07	.14	-.07
		guilt	.50*	.30*	.33*	.27*
	T=2	moral behavior	.04	.19	.26*	.10
		guilt	-.11	.10	.16	.22
cohort 2	T=1	moral behavior	.02	-.01	.11	-.07
		guilt	.29*	.33*	-.01	.16
	T=2	moral behavior	.11	-.10	.10	.24
		guilt	-.03	-.12	.26*	.17
cohort 3	T=1	moral behavior	.01	.08	-.06	.10
		guilt	.57*	.18	.48	.07
	T=2	moral behavior	.02	-.25	.03	.01
		guilt	.37*	.32*	.23*	.44*

Note The number of subjects within each subsample are:
72 boys with 72 mothers and 62 fathers
78 girls with 78 mothers and 70 fathers
cohort 1: 47 children, 47 mothers, 42 fathers
cohort 2: 50 children, 50 mothers, 45 fathers
cohort 3: 53 children, 53 mothers, 45 fathers
* p < .05

CURRICULUM VITAE

Anke de Veer (geboren te Eindhoven, 1959) behaalde in 1977 het diploma Atheneum-B. In 1985 studeerde zij af in de Psychologie aan de Katholieke Universiteit Nijmegen (ontwikkelingspsychologie en psychologische functieleer). Vanaf 1986 was zij verbonden aan de vakgroep Algemene Pedagogiek van de Katholieke Universiteit Nijmegen, waar zij het in dit proefschrift beschreven onderzoek uitvoerde. Sinds 1987 is zij als docente werkzaam bij de Katholieke Leergangen Tilburg, bij de opleiding pedagogiek. Vanaf juli 1990 is zij als onderzoekster werkzaam bij de Stichting NIVEL te Utrecht.